A Free Catholicism
for the
Third Millennium

Introduction to the
Philosophy and Charism of the
Ascension Alliance

By Thomas J. Hickey
Edited by Alan R. Kemp

Hermitage Desktop Press
Vaughn, Washington

A Free Catholicism
for the
Third Millennium

Introduction to the
Philosophy and Charism of the
Ascension Alliance

By Thomas J. Hickey
Edited by Alan R. Kemp

Copyright © 2015 Ascension Alliance

All rights reserved. No part of this book may be reproduced by any means, graphic, electronic or mechanical including photocopying, taping or by any informational storage retrieval system without written permission of the publisher except in cases of brief quotations embodied in critical articles or reviews. For additional information please contact the publisher:

Hermitage Desktop Press
P.O. Box 167
Vaughn, WA 98394

ISBN: 9780692437995

Printed in the United States of America

Table of Contents

Editor's Note vi

Preface viii

An Overview 2
Independent 2
Mystical 5
Reformed 7
Liberal 11
Catholic 16
Spiritual and Religious 20
Love 22
Eclectic 23
Pluralistic 24

Our Approach to the Spiritual Journey 26
Modern and Traditional 37
Our Liberal Tradition 41
Spiritual Science 45
Purpose 50

The Primacy of the Spiritual and Mystical 56
Esoteric 57
Metaphysical 63
God 68
One True Path? 74
Christian Unity 75
Christology 77
Apostolic 85

Sacraments and Sacramentals 92
Holy Eucharist 95
Absolution 97
Holy Unction and Healing 101
Holy Matrimony 104
Baptism 106
Confirmation 108
Holy Orders 110

Liturgy	125
Scripture	131
Tradition	135
Theology and Philosophy	138
Christian Ethics	147
Fellowship In The Spirit	152
Epilogue	154
ABOUT ASCENSION	156

Editor's Note

This is a fifth edition of Thomas J. Hickey's original book on independent Catholicism. This insightful work was first published 1989. It was revised and edited in 1998 by the present editor, a process that resulted in the publication of a second edition. In that edition, the word 'mystic' and 'mystical' was used in lieu of the more ecclesiastically charged word 'gnostic' and 'gnosticism' that appeared in the original. The reason for the change was to clarify that the sponsoring organization did not specifically adopt gnostic doctrines, which critics had erroneously charged. Rather, those terms were used to refer to a more generalized spiritual knowing. In the third edition only cosmetic changes, like typeface, were made.

The fourth edition was the result of a process of reflection and discernment about the nature, purpose, and goals of the Ascension Alliance, which has since adopted it. This book was approved as an introduction to the philosophy and charism of the Ascension Ascension – one branch of the Mystical Body of Christ. The author, Thomas J. Hickey, had given us permission to edit the book for this purpose and to distribute it for nonprofit religious and educational purposes.

In the present volume, we have attempted to clean up minor errors and to publish an edition that is professionally formatted and printed, using the resources of CreateSpace and "on-demand" publishing.

From the standpoint of the Ascension Alliance and Community of Ascensionists, the book you are now holding has the equivalent of the *nihil obstat* and *imprimatur* of the Alliance. In other words, nothing should stand in the way of its being published and we believe that it is free from doctrinal errors. It is thereby authorized for use by the Ascension Alliance, the Community of Ascensionists, its clergy, and all of its affiliated ministries.

Preface

"When I was a graduate student at Harvard ... I wanted to find the 'real Christianity' – and I assumed I could find it by going back to the earliest Christians ... What I found was the opposite of what I expected. What I did not find in the process of this research was what I had started out to find – a 'golden age' of purer and simpler early Christianity. What I discovered instead is that the 'real Christianity' – so far as historical investigation can disclose it – was not monolithic, or the province of one party or other, but included a variety of voices, and an extraordinary range of viewpoints ... From a strictly historical viewpoint, then, there is no single 'real Christianity.'"

– Elaine Pagels
Adam, Eve and the Serpent

An Overview

This book uses a broad brush to paint a picture of our movement that is neither merely a caricature, nor yet a detailed analysis. It is intended primarily to acquaint the reader with an approach to religion and spirituality inspired by a vision of a free Catholicism, inspired by the intuitions of the "Independent Catholic," "Emerging Church," and "Jewish Renewal" movements.

INDEPENDENT

Why do we speak of an independent Catholicism? Christianity has experienced significant reformations several times over the course of its development, due to historical and cultural pressures. A reformation occurred, for example, in the transition of the early Christian community from predominantly Jewish to predominantly Gentile, when the Christian message came to be interpreted in a cultural context quite different from that of its inception.

Another significant reformation occurred when Christianity became the official religion of the Roman Empire and an orthodoxy sanctioned by political supremacy all but obliterated the rich diversity that early Christianity had known. Of course, the Protestant Reformation is now popularly considered to be the most significant to date, when the reformers went their separate ways.

Historically, we may view the Protestant Reformation as the almost inevitable cultural consequence of the Renaissance, which heralded the end of the Middle Ages. Reawakened awareness of classical antiquity, the rise of the middle class that signaled the demise of medieval feudalism, along with growing European nationalism, contributed to a social milieu that ushered in drastic changes. The very roots of Christianity were shaken, in reaction to the behavior of the medieval Church as successor of the Roman Empire. Moreover, technological and scientific advancement, especially the invention of the printing press, played no small part in the development and dissemination of new ideas.

Christianity is at another similar juncture in its development at this time, owing principally to the vast growth of knowledge, improved methodology, as well as the speed of its transmission, and because of advanced technology. No less an important influence is the shrinking of the world, owing to advances in communications and transportation technology, with the result that a single world culture is developing.

In the field of religion, for example, biblical research and archeological discoveries are revealing that the popular conception of the Gospels as entirely inspired revelations, or even as true historical records, is untenable. However, advances in scholarly research have not yet come to public attention and a "pious fraud" continues to be perpetrated through the pulpits. We see an inevitable revolution in the making as "orthodoxy" attempts to stave off inevitable change.

At least three major reactions can be predicted. Some will persist in holding to accustomed beliefs, even in the face of the evidence. This group will gradually die out, however, surviving, if at all, as a living fossil. Others will view the evidence as indeed revolutionary and abandon any pretext of Christian belief, in favor of material complacency, scientific humanism, or some different form of spirituality. A third is to participate in the building of a reformed

Catholicism, adapting what is spiritually efficacious to our evolving cultural conditions, newly discovered historical realities, and promising future possibilities.

The anthropomorphic concept of God is dead for most intelligent people. Furthermore, given contemporary biblical studies, it is no longer possible to maintain that the entire Torah was dictated to Moses by Yahweh, that the prophets were inspired such that they spoke independently of cultural and historical conditioning, or that the Gospels are either predominantly historical records or biographical accounts (rather than chiefly confessional and kerygmatic works).

In addition, biological, anthropological and sociological knowledge of the process of evolution is giving rise to a new conception of humanity, just as advances in the physical sciences are revolutionizing our conceptualizations about the universe, and technology is making possible the transformation of our environment. A new global worldview is being born, and it is radically different than the one many of us were educated about just a few short decades ago.

We seek to meet the challenge of these rather sweeping cultural changes by preserving our sacramental Christian traditions, the deep spiritual insights which we experience as a source of spiritual empowerment, while recognizing that the conceptual models we have used to structure our religious ideas may need to be expanded in the light of maturing knowledge.

Moreover, we are willing to revisit, reexamine, the "heresies" and other heterodoxies in a new light, realizing that something of what they contain may prove useful to us now. For we have come to see that many of the decisions made earlier regarding orthodoxy and canon may have been influenced more by cultural conditions than had been previously realized. Perhaps the other sides of the great controversies deserve a fresh "hearing," especially in light of new knowledge and more mature attitudes. Pelagius and Nestorius, for example, make telling points that seem to deserve more consideration than an offhanded dismissal.

MYSTICAL

We would agree with Mircea Eliade, who remarks in the preface to his book, *A History of Religious Ideas*, that "the 'sacred' is an element in the structure of consciousness and not a stage in the history of consciousness … In other words, to be – or, rather, to become – a human being signifies being 'religious.'" The Ascension Alliance exists to provide an alternative for the person who wishes to continue to express religious dimensions of consciousness through traditional sacramental worship, and yet wants to approach the sacred in a way that befits contemporary human intelligence.

We know from the latest developments in physics that the universe is made up of one "stuff," which scientists have come to call "energy," and interestingly, energy is also a term that emphasizes the power to produce change. However, contemporary scientific thinking holds that latent information directs change in regular patterns and is as fundamental as energy, if not even more basic. Indeed, for many, the beauty in contemporary physics lies in observing how a single elementary force unfolds into a universe of growing complexity, in accordance with the information latent in the initial singularity, as the original fireball rapidly expands and its temperature falls.

In light of the Big Bang theory, it seems that the history of the universe is a sequential unfoldment of increasing complexity from an initial singularity, brought about by a process of symmetry breaking. We ourselves, as configurations of congealed energy, were already contained in this initial state as "information," so to speak, waiting to unfold in a drama involving the elaboration of our "structure," both material and psychic. From human and religious points of view, we prefer to call this information "intelligence."

There is an ongoing debate as to whether consciousness is fundamental to existence, or is "merely" an emergent property of an unfolding universe. It is beyond the scope of this work to enter into the ramifications of this debate. Suffice it to say that it is possible to experience consciousness as fundamental to existence. We may postulate, then, that the structure of the one original "stuff" contains as an integral aspect the structure of consciousness. Furthermore, we may say, along with Jung, that the structure of consciousness itself contains many structures, of which the sacred may be a primary one. We submit that the aspect of consciousness that enables us to discover structure, both our own and that of the universe, is the sacred, for it is this which is the holistic, or the "holy."

An analysis of contemporary religious thinking, might suggest that consciousness becoming more and more aware of itself is the foundation for a truly mystical spirituality. This state of being aware – energy becoming progressively awake to its own existence – as well as its inherent intelligence in and through us, may be what we can profitably call "mystical knowledge."

Our orientation *is* mystical in the sense of being directed to uncovering "the holy" that is within. We take it as a fundamental message of Christianity that "The kingdom of God is within you." We interpret this message as prophetic of the development of human spirituality in the Third Millennium, as universal evolution proceeds to ever greater elaboration as expressed through our science, art, the humanities, religion, and the spiritual experience itself.

REFORMED

But is this orthodox? The etymology of the word suggests its meaning to be 'right thinking.' According to one dictionary, 'orthodox' in religion means "according to established doctrine." While we respect church tradition, we establish no doctrine as sacrosanct; holding instead that knowledge is ever growing, so we must consider ourselves to be reformed rather than orthodox.

Why do we prescind from established doctrine? There are several reasons underlying this choice. Fundamental to every religion is a philosophy, that is, "a way of life." Our contemporary Christian way of life is drastically different culturally from the first century Jewish way of life, into which Christianity was born, far different from the medieval way of life in which it flourished, and different from prescientific Christianity.

Personal freedom has become a basic feature of our way of life in the West, since the advent of political democracy. This freedom is grounded in the availability of universal education, which gives individuals the ability to assume personal responsibility. Those who feel qualified to assume personal responsibility demand the personal freedom to exercise it. Those who are willing to mindfully accept responsibility for themselves do not take kindly to "orthodoxies," in which there is little room for personal insight and initiative.

Basic to the Christian philosophy is that human beings have "free will," that is the freedom to choose among options for action, together with the faculty of conscience to direct this choice by using proper means to attain worthy ends.

This philosophical view, not found in other cultures, at least as explicitly, is now a fundamental part of our Western way of life. Our present concept of freedom owes much to the cultural conditions out of which Christianity arose.

In the first place, Christianity placed emphasis on the notion that personal salvation is dependent on a person's internal condition, more than on the external condition of conforming to a complex set of cultural conditions, such as the Jewish Law came to be interpreted, according to the Gospel accounts. Judging from the Gospels, Jesus was preaching a reformed Judaism against the "orthodoxy" of the time when he taught that the spirit of the Law is love, and that the spirit prevails over the letter, that is, the precepts. Secondly, early Christianity was a reaction against Roman tyranny throughout the ancient world. While political freedom seemed impossible to attain in the face of Roman might, spiritual freedom was available to all who had the faith to commit to it. The early Christians believed that baptism so transformed a person as to make spiritual freedom a reality. No longer constrained by "original sin" a person could behave responsibly.

The "orthodox" view, however, is that original sin permanently condemns humanity to moral weakness, called "concupiscence." Only God's grace can redeem human beings and this grace is mediated by the Church He instituted. In this view, our responsibility is to follow "orthodoxy" and not trust to conscience.

How did this denial of personal freedom and responsibility come about? In the book, *Adam, Eve and the Serpent*, Elaine Pagels seeks to show that it was the influential Augustine who, unable to control his own strong passions, argued persuasively that this is a universal and permanent addiction of mankind.

Why was the orthodox church ready to accept this reversal of the earlier, and apparently more Christian position? Pagels points out that the cultural milieu had shifted drastically. The orthodox church had come to be the official religion of the Roman Empire and enjoyed the sanction of the state. Rival views were no longer tolerated and Augustine's argument provided a philosophical basis for insisting that the church "magisterium" was morally determinative, not individual conscience.

By the time of the Inquisition, "orthodoxy" had become the problem it had purportedly solved. While the Protestant Reformation attempted to correct the situation, the reformers dismantled the sacramental system and instituted an orthodoxy of the Bible that has flowered as Fundamentalism.

However, contemporary biblical research reveals

that the established doctrines and interpretations, based on traditional views of the scriptures are no longer tenable by intelligent people.

Pagels points out that Augustine's view of original sin may be based on a misreading of Genesis. Similarly, doctrines and theologies which appeal to the scriptures must now be reexamined in the light of contemporary research – historical, biblical, linguistic, and scientific.

The clergy are, so to speak, doctors of the soul. As such they are professionals with a high degree of responsibility. When we become ill we consult professional medical practitioners, confident that they are conversant with the state of the art in their profession. To be less than highly qualified, opens them to the charge of negligence.

Clergy are no less a professional class and are just as responsible for keeping informed as any professional. The clergy of many "orthodox" institutions, however, are either not conversant with contemporary findings, or they are silent about them to their people.

Why would the "orthodox" churches resist the evidence growing from rigorous investigation? Traditions often persist long after their period of appropriateness, due to the inertia of the prevailing cultural world view. Well-meaning clergy are either themselves the victims of this collective thought form or they continue to perpetrate a "pious fraud," so as not to upset their congregations. In addition, a whole set of vested interests are involved.

Herein lies the necessity for a reinvigorated Catholic church. Those who experience the spiritual power of the sacraments do not wish to give them up; yet, they also wish to avail themselves of the best thinking of the time. They wish to educate themselves, so as best to meet the challenge of personal responsibility that freedom of choice involves.

As a body, we should take responsibility for our growth, within the context of a valid sacramental tradition, and with access to the best resources for personal development. Just as Jesus was at the cutting edge of his time, so are we called to be on the forefront of knowledge in our own.

LIBERAL

We have just considered the dichotomy between the orthodox and the reformed approaches. An equally important distinction is between conservative and the liberal approaches.

Here it may be fruitful to distinguish between different expressions of fundamentalism and liberalism. Protestant Fundamentalism, the position that the Bible is literally true, and Catholic Fundamentalism, the position that the Holy Spirit directly inspires both scripture and tradition, and that the ultimate arbiter is the "magisterium" of the Church.

In both cases, the individual is positioned secondary to a dogmatic conception of truth which is not merely a guide, but also a constraint. The value of this position lies in the uniformity it guarantees, as well as the psychological security of the rigidly established structure it provides.

Unfortunately, many fundamentalists either fail to recognize or conveniently forget that their certainty is that of belief and not of knowledge. In their enthusiasm, they often seek to impose the structure they have accepted on others, who may, for example, be under the sway of either liberal theology or scientific humanism.

Liberals and humanists, on the other hand, point to research which strongly suggests that fundamentalism is in many instances in contradiction to a reasonable and intelligent position. It is difficult to maintain in the face of the evidence that the world was created a few thousand years ago, or that the evolution of species did not take place.

But even with respect to the scriptures themselves and the tradition of the church, there are problem areas. Contemporary biblical and archeological research strongly supports the position that the scriptures were authored by human beings whose religious concerns were bound up in the social and political situation of the times. In addition, the traditionally accepted authors of scripture are often found not to be the actual authors.

Unfortunately, a great deal of this research has been confined to scholarly publications and has not filtered into the public consciousness. However, recently some excellent work is being made available in a more popular form. For example, *Who Wrote The Bible* by Richard Elliott Friedman, a graduate of Harvard's prestigious program in Hebrew studies, is a fascinating account of the currents that affected the composition of the Pentateuch, showing how the discrepancies in the text reveal different authorship with conflicting social and political intentions. So too, in Catholic circles, where tradition is accepted as equally valid as scripture, fundamentalists and liberals are contending. Claiming the force of tradition, for example, conservatives reject the contention that women are qualified for orders, while liberals argue that this prejudice against women is simply another instance of cultural bias.

A cardinal tenet of Catholic fundamentalism is the doctrine of original sin, an ancient Hebrew notion that explains human suffering and natural imperfection on the basis of guilt. Christ's suffering, then, becomes both the example for good Christians, making their own suffering bearable, and also the expiation of spiritual guilt, so that suffering for the faithful is believed to be limited to this earthly life and to "purgatory," a merely temporary state in the eternal afterlife.

Of course, the essence of the Catholic fundamentalist position is the infallibility of the teaching "magisterium" of the Church, epitomized in the doctrine of the infallibility of the Pope when speaking formally on matters of faith and morals.

Again, the value of the fundamentalist position lies in the solidity that unquestionable belief lends to the structure through which its adherents relate to their world. Whatever the problem or difficulty, there is a clear answer to it.

As the great social scientist, Malinowski pointed out, religion as a social institution is functional. That is to say, religion is a cultural phenomenon that answers specific needs of the particular culture, just as does its governmental system, its educational system and its legal system. In fact, in more primitive cultures all these functions are bound together in the culture as a single institution.

Religion has traditionally been the carrier of philosophy, understood as the foundation for a cultural way of life. For fundamentalists, this remains true. Their religion, in addition to being a form of worship and spiritual development, also embodies the philosophical structure that gives its adherents a secure place in an ever changing Universe.

Theological liberals and secular humanists, on the other hand, find it difficult, if not impossible, to put their faith in scriptural interpretations and traditions which no longer seem viable in the light of contemporary scholarship.

Religion takes on a different function for them. Religion is no longer looked upon as more than a form of worship and a means of spiritual development.

Thus, the liberal position, while being intellectually freer, is less secure emotionally. Those who reserve for themselves freedom of choice on the basis of intelligent deliberation accept the responsibility for creating their own world. There is no infallible structure to rely on. They must decide for themselves what seems most reasonable, on the basis of informed research and dialogue, – a momentous responsibility.

While fundamentalists reinforce each others' belief system with their primarily emotional relation to religion, liberals serve each other as sounding-boards for intelligent investigation and dialogue. The amount of information today makes it impossible for any one person, or even a few people, to keep up to date in a single discipline, let alone in anything as multifaceted as the study of all that impacts religion and philosophy.

While freedom from dogmatic bonds may be invigorating for the liberal at first blush, the resulting responsibility, based upon the freedom of choice among many options, can be intimidating. The temptation is always to slip back into yet another aspect of fundamentalism in order to gain that security of structure which had to be given up to gain freedom from dogmatism.

Revolutionaries typically crystallize once their revolution is won, and they bind their children in bonds as tight as those they broke. Taking heed from their example, liberals need to bear in mind the true meaning of liberalism which is not so much *freedom from* dogmatism as it is *freedom for* self-determination.

Liberals hold that human beings do not come with an operating manual precisely because all must discover their own essence and potential within. The experience of others is there as a guide, but only as a guide. Each one must come to his or her own conclusions regarding the meaning and purpose of life, and how best to accomplish it.

The experience of the past is a guide for the future, and religious traditions are useful in helping us to come to an intelligent appraisal of fundamental options. There are many such guides, however, and all too often people simply grow up in a tradition which they inherit, so to speak, and never question. They seem to be unaware that there might be better suited alternatives, even though there are major discrepancies between their inherited beliefs and their own natural inclinations.

CATHOLIC

Our approach is one option among many expressions of Christianity. Although the organization is open and non-credal, it is an alternative among the many larger and more influential sacramental churches which count themselves Catholic or Orthodox.

The denominations of the Christian Church are customarily divided into Catholic, Orthodox, and Protestant. Catholicism is often equated with the Roman Catholic Church and the rites in communion with it, while other western Christian churches are called Protestant. However, there are rites which are independent of Rome and which are also properly called Catholic.

What differentiates Protestantism from Catholicism is not communion with the Roman Church, as many believe. Actually, Christian churches may be classified depending on whether they perform the sacramental rites in accordance with tradition and conform to the apostolic succession of Holy Orders.

Of the sacramental churches observing the apostolic succession of Holy Orders, there are two major branches, the Catholic tradition of the West and the Orthodox tradition of the East. The separation was at first political occurring when Constantine removed the capital of the empire to Constantinople.

Since Rome had for so long been the imperial city, it was natural that the Bishop of Rome would enjoy the imperial reputation, even after the emperor had left. Subsequently the bishops of Rome and Constantinople contested with each other, until the inevitable break, with each side excommunicating the other.

The historical result is that the eastern, or Orthodox, church and the western, or Catholic church, have developed different liturgies, while maintaining the same sacraments and belief in the importance of apostolic succession. Among the sacramental and apostolic churches, there are many rites, differentiated by doctrine, liturgy, and canon, but united by their agreement on the requirements for sacramental efficacy.

The eastern Orthodox churches have been less monolithic historically than the western Catholic Church, due largely to the fact that the absence of the emperor in Rome (who now took up residence in eastern Constantinople), which left a vacuum which the Bishop of Rome was in an ideal position to fill. Thus, the imperial mantle fell to the shoulders of the pope more as a sociological phenomenon than as a religious dictate.

In the East there have traditionally been a plethora of rites, loosely in communion, while in the Latin West a single monolithic organization tended to dominate the scene until the Protestant Reformation. At the time of the Reformation, corruption in the church led to the formation of different denominations, rather than merely different rites, as the reformers rejected the sacramental tradition whose efficacy is dependent upon the apostolic succession, and a priestly class who controlled it. The ministry of the priesthood was rejected, in favor of the direct and personal relationship of each person to God through the mediation of Jesus Christ himself, as he is revealed to the world in the Gospels.

Nonetheless, in the Roman Catholic tradition there are a multiplicity of rites, all of whom recognize each other as valid expressions of catholicity, since they conform to the essentials of the sacramental tradition and the preservation of the apostolic succession of their Holy Orders. The Latin rite, while dominant, is but one of many held to be legitimate within the Roman Catholic Church. Many outside the Roman Catholic Church consider themselves equally "catholic." For example, many in the Anglican Church, consider it to be essentially a Catholic rite, rather than a Protestant church, even though it may have been a phenomenon that emerged from the Protestant Reformation.

A further break in the monolithic Roman Church came into fruition in the later decades of the nineteenth century, when factions of the Dutch, German, and Swiss Catholic churches declared their independence from Rome over the issue of papal infallibility that was declared at the First Vatican Council. They formed the Union of Utrecht, which continues to exist as a Catholic communion independent of the authority and jurisdiction of the Roman pontiff. Such churches call themselves "Old Catholic," maintaining a Catholic orientation in matters of faith, and preserving their apostolic succession. In addition, there are a number of independent, ancient, and apostolic churches which are primarily ethnic in their composition and liturgies.

Ours is an independent Church in the Catholic tradition in a similar sense. Our liturgy observes the essentials of the Catholic sacramental tradition and our orders are valid by virtue of having carefully preserved our apostolic succession.

The Ascension movement is Catholic in another sense also. For we are critical rather than dogmatic with respect to doctrine and theology. Whereas the Roman Church claims a divine *"magisterium"* or teaching authority, capped by the rather embarrassing doctrine of papal infallibility, we emphasize individual responsibility, based on freedom of conscience. Ascension Alliance is a liberal organization, rather than a magisterial one: we support people and encourage people *to* think, but not *what* to think, or *how*.

The underlying principle is that human nature is oriented toward progress: the universal creative spirit that is responsible for evolution leads sincere people to greater self development, provided they are given the freedom to unfold their potential as they see fit. Of course, guidance is necessary on the path, and education properly plays the role of a guide, but not of a master.

In our view, freedom is ultimately "freedom for," rather than primarily "freedom from" or "freedom to." That is to say, the fundamental purpose of freedom is for unfolding one's inherent potential i.e., developing excellence. In order to pursue this goal a person should be free from intervening constraint and free to explore the range of possibility. Freedom is not a matter of caprice or license, but is a necessary condition for self-actualization.

The word, "catholic," means 'universal.' We hold that driving force of evolution is universal to existence, and that it impels human beings to self discovery. Therefore, we hold that if a church is to truly deserve the name "Catholic," it should orient itself to promoting the evolutionary drive toward

Self-realization by creating the conditions which foster the unfolding of self-actualization. Therefore, in our estimation, independence, in the sense of "freedom for self-actualization," is integral to spirituality, properly conceived.

SPIRITUAL AND RELIGIOUS

In this regard, we also distinguish between the spiritual and the religious. Spirituality is openness to transcendence. Religion is oriented to divine worship.

Although spirituality and religion are thought of as going hand in hand, this is not necessarily the case. If religious conceptions do not promote transcendence, then spirituality may be lacking in the religion's adherents. Or again, one may be extremely spiritual without being obviously religious. The stricter Buddhists, for example, are highly spiritual, but may not be religious at all.

Ascension differentiates between the spiritual and the religious, by recalling that the function of the priest is to perform the sacred rites, a religious function. Ordination is the necessary and sufficient condition for sacramental efficacy, along with proper performance of the liturgy.

Spiritual guidance, however, is the province of those who have successfully trod the path. Ordination and liturgical worship by themselves do not automatically result in spiritual adeptship. Therefore, Ascension encourages all seekers to adopt any and all spiritual means they find appropriate, regardless of the tradition from which they come.

We maintain that evolution is a universal spiritual phenomenon and that all peoples and all cultures are expressions of this primary force in the direction of transcendence. Entering the third millennium, we are witnessing the dawn of a globalization of humanity. All cultures are influencing each other and a common world culture is arising.

While individual religions are preserving their traditions of divine worship, a technology of spirituality is being formulated which transcends the vagaries of sect and creed. Ascension, as an independent rite, is maintaining an ancient religious tradition while providing an alternative for those taking personal responsibility for their spiritual development. Hence, we seek to incorporate the best resources for spiritual growth.

Ascension presents the option of offering divine worship in a Catholic tradition, while also positioning one's self on the cutting edge of human spiritual evolution in our time. The world now needs people to get involved in creating an appropriate spirituality and appropriate religions, in addition to appropriate educational systems, appropriate politics, appropriate economics and appropriate technology.

Spirituality and religions are concerned primarily with the distribution of spiritual power, of course, yet sociologically they serve the function of transmitting personal and cultural values. Values are determinative with respect to all choices made by individuals and cultures; therefore, values are determinative of all personal expression and cultural activity. With a global culture fast developing, we stand in a unique place at this time in history to shape the future by the seeds we plant now. We believe this should be aspirational rather than dogmatic. As noted religionist, Houston Smith, suggests that religion is the institutionalization of spirituality. In keeping with the insights of the Emerging Church movement, we now strive to deconstruct old institutions that no longer work and re-create ourselves as an expression of the stirrings of Spirit today.

At a deep personal level *spiritual alchemy* is the transformation of ordinary states of human consciousness into holistic awareness. This is what "religion," meaning 'to bind back' (to source), was ultimately concerned with. The religion of the future may be more purely spiritual, oriented to the discovery of divinity within. Actually, the religion of the future is always just another revival of the ancient, indeed primordial spirituality in a form and terminology suitable for the time. In this regard, those on the cutting edge are really only translators for the Higher Self.

LOVE

As a mystically oriented Christian church, Ascension strives to embody a "heart yoga," a path of spiritual transformation through the power of love. The particular contribution of Christianity to the development of world spirituality is that the way to the kingdom of God is not predominantly through the head, nor through the hands, but rather through the heart.

Asked the essence of the Law, Jesus quoted the Law itself when he replied: "Love the Lord your God with your whole heart your whole mind and your whole strength; and love your neighbor as yourself. This is the whole of the Law and the prophets" (Deuteronomy 6:4-5; Leviticus 19:18; Matthew 22:35-40). St. John elaborates: "God is love. Those who abide in love abide in God and God abides in them" (1 John 4:16). St. Augustine sees even Christian ethics as love-based rather than law-based, in his famous dictum: "Anna et fac quod vis," i.e., 'Love and do as you will.' His reasoning is, if one acts completely from unconditional love, what can one do but good?

ECLECTIC

Much Catholic, Orthodox and Protestant religious expression has for a long time been centered on sin, guilt and suffering, rather than on increasing love in one's self and in the world, and has emphasized Messianic redemption for salvation after death over and at the expense of spiritual development for mystical enlightenment here and now. We have sought to purify our theology and liturgy of these limiting aspects.

We have set the focus strongly on the positive. From the charismatic, we have adopted the stance that the mark of the original Christians was that they were quite obviously "spirit-filled." From the mystics, we have gleaned the availability of divine wisdom in this life. From the traditionalists, we have the sacramental rites and the apostolic succession of Holy Orders that grounds their efficacy. From the metaphysicians, we have come to see the sacraments as instances of Christian *"sacred magic,"* as it were, which provide for the distribution of spiritual power both in the person and in the environment as well – in a way that is real and palpable for those with spiritually refined perception. From other spiritual religious, mystical and metaphysical traditions, we have derived further theory and technology of the sacred, such as uplifting expressions, spiritual exercises and meditative practices.

Although we approach Christian tradition anew, we do not see ourselves as innovators; for "there is nothing new under the sun." We seek to combine creatively the tried and true in a way suitable for our times, and we present a focus that is appropriate for the type of people we are. If you feel you are one of us, we wholeheartedly welcome you: "Let birds of a feather flock together." We are aware that we may be criticized as being "unconventional" by those who adhere to rigidly established traditions and interpretations. Yet, we would point out that Jesus himself was criticized for being too unconventional, especially by those who believed they were the arbiters of God's word. Moreover, what little we know of the early church suggests that it attracted the unconventional rather than appealing to the pillars of society of the time. In fact, it wasn't until the persecutions were over and the church was raised to imperial status that it became a bastion of conventionality.

PLURALISTIC

We are pluralists who believe that our way is best for us, and that there is no absolutely "best" way for all. Our only disagreement is with those who attempt to force their way on others who do not choose it voluntarily as the most suitable option for them. The fact that there are literally thousands of different denominations of Christianity alone, not to mention all the other religions of the world and their numerous sects, shows that there are about as many ways of following the Lord as there are different types of people. It's our position, if everyone would get with their own kind and recognize the right of others to think, express themselves, and worship as they wish, there would be a lot more peace on earth.

In conclusion, what is presented herein does not represent a dogmatic statement, or prescription about what members must believe. Rather, it should be read as a general description of our beliefs, understanding, and aspirations. The late Patriarch and Matriarch of the Church of Antioch, as well as several bishops of that church, read the manuscript at various stages of its development, and offered valuable suggestions to the first edition. The author thanks the late Patriarch, Archbishop Herman Adrian Spruit, and our late Matriarch, Archbishop Meri Louise Spruit, Bishop Timothy Barker, Bishop Howard Dugan, and especially his mother, Emma, and his spouse, the Reverend Janet Louise, for their support and contributions. Special acknowledgment goes to Bishop Paul Clemens, publisher at Blue Dolphin Publishing, Inc., of Nevada City, California, for his valuable editorial services on the first edition. This fifth edition was reviewed by the editor.

We believe that this summary is a fair representation of what many informed members of our organization take to be its particular character. We hope it may also serve as a useful guide for those interested in our approach to spirituality in the third millennium.

Finally, we should reiterate that ours is only one expression of a more universal movement toward spiritual renewal. We join with all our brothers and sisters of whatever creed in Spirit and in the hope that our aspirations will converge and help bring about mutual understanding and greater Peace in the World. It is hope of our organization that this edition may make at least a small contribution in furthering these aims.

Our Approach to the Spiritual Journey

The Ascension movement is principally mystical, metaphysical, sacramental, and liberal rather than canonical or doctrinal. Instead of espousing a particular doctrine as a condition for membership, or requiring conformity to a set of precepts, Ascension holds itself forth as a fertile field in which the Spirit can unfold itself in human hearts by means of interior spiritual experience, esoteric symbolism, metaphysical practice, sacramental grace and initiation.

While no specific orientation is required for membership, many clergy and members are mystical in the broad sense, that is, they understand divinity as something to be experienced directly. Therefore, proper religious methodology consists not only of divine worship, but also of spiritual science, since a principal purpose of religion is to provide both intellectual appreciation and experiential knowledge.

Spiritual science is the disclosing of eternal mysteries within one's self in accordance with tested principles. Every manifestation of the one, true, unmanifest way is a mystery religion, in the sense that spiritual truth can only be hinted at in words and symbols because it can only be grasped in its totality. Wholeness of knowledge is available only to those in a state of holistic awareness. Spiritual development is the unfolding of holistic awareness which transforms the mysteries of religion into spiritual science.

Ascension approaches religion as the methodology of spiritual science, as well as a medium for divine worship. The word, "religion," means "to bind back." Religions exist to bind their people back to the infinite Source. There is no good to be derived from arguing about which religion is superior, since all religions are cultural manifestations of the unmanifest Truth. Since there is only one Source, there is essentially only one interior path, although it manifests historically under many cultural guises, "as different caravans on the way."

Moreover, on the path there are many personality types, each with its own natural tendencies and predilections. Those who are predominantly intellectual may emphasize the way of discrimination, while people of the heart may prefer the way of devotion. Those who are predominantly oriented to activity may emphasize the way of selfless service, while those who are more contemplative may emphasize internal techniques, such as prayer, contemplation, and meditation. Those who are more solitary may pursue the life of the monk, while those who are more gregarious may follow the life of the householder.

There are many ways for spirituality to unfold itself. Not only may different people choose different orientations, but also, individuals may employ different foci simultaneously, or change focus over the course of their development.

What is good for one person or culture is not necessarily good for all. Each must find his or her own way by following the promptings of the Spirit within. However, since no one is an island, common themes arise given similar sociological situations, and the groupings of individuals sharing specific traits form the various religions and the sects therein.

The Ascension organization claims no "magisterium" or supernatural guarantee of doctrinal purity. The ultimate justification in religious matters is neither historical nor scriptural, neither philosophical nor theological neither magisterial nor doctrinal. Spiritual proof is internal as the *self-authority of the God within*. It is the spiritual power that comes from "supernatural grace," as it has been called, the divine love that flows from the devotion of a pure heart and the metaphysical transcendence that derives from correct spiritual practice.

Each of us is here to help each other unfold Truth to ourselves in the only place it can be known and – within. For 'Truth' signifies "holistic awareness." Once this Truth is gained, it cannot be imparted to others save by assisting others to find it within themselves as their very nature.

If the Truth could be spoken out or written down and be clearly understood, then well informed and well-intentioned people would no longer disagree. However, scripture and tradition, as well as the words of the great saints, mystics, philosophers and theologians, remain open to interpretation, and interpretation is relative to one's level of intelligence, experience and spiritual achievement.

As we employ it, the term "spiritual" means "open to transcendence." Language based on conceptual understanding can never grasp the spiritual dimension, but merely serves to point in a direction. The danger in interpreting spiritual and religious language lies in mistaking the finger for the moon at which it is pointing. Poets and prophets, mystics and theologians simply point the way. It is up to individuals to walk the path and to discover the goal for themselves. Scripture is cited herein not by way of proving a claim, nor even to support a conviction. Every reading of a text involves interpretation, especially when the meaning is complex and the intention of the original uttered is involved. Scripture is far from obvious, due both to the richness of levels of interpretation and to the fact that biblical research is far from conclusive on many fundamental issues. Moreover, new discoveries, such as the *Dead Sea Scrolls* and the *Nag Hammadi Library,* have altered the fundamental ground.

In addition, new techniques of scholarship are modifying previous theories, bringing the authenticity of many traditional texts and interpretations into question, and adding credence to the relevance of non-canonical texts and non-orthodox interpretations. For example, contemporary New Testament scholars are generally in agreement that the pre-Easter historical material concerning the life and ministry of Jesus has been edited and shaped to conform to the post-Easter theological perspective.

Anyone familiar with the volume of scriptural exegesis and the difficulties involved in discriminating among competing claims realizes that, for the most part, scripture itself is in need of proof. Most importantly, however, scripture needs proving in ourselves through our spiritual unfoldment.

Compounding the difficulty of scriptural interpretation is the discovery of ancient manuscripts that show the early church growing out of a variety of influences and positions, only one of which in the West, called "Catholic," emerged victorious after the fray. The victorious party, representing an authoritarian and hierarchical clergy, a dogmatic creed and an institutionalized religion, decreed the canon of scripture and a dogmatic theology to suit its own ends. The victors sought to annihilate competing positions, and to extirpate all record of their existence, except as reported by the official "heresiologists," i.e., their own historians who specialized in what those who had declared themselves orthodox labeled "heresies." "Heretics" were persecuted with the ferocity the Romans had used against the early Christians and their books were burnt.

A major competing position was the gnostic. "Gnostic" is related etymologically to "know," and it means spiritual knowledge. Gnostics as discrete groups held a variety of specific theological positions. Gnosticism, in the broad sense of the term, however, underlies the mystical dimensions of virtually every religion. Oriental religions, such as Hinduism, Buddhism and Taoism are more open about their mysticism, but occidental religions have been more dominated by the exoteric element, requiring its mystics to be more circumspect.

That is to say, Eastern religions, like Hinduism, Taoism, and Buddhism, either were less dominated by the mass consciousness that focuses on the trappings of religion, rather than on the spiritual essence, or at least were tolerant of those who pursued the spiritual path successfully and were wont to report on it. Western religions, like Judaism, Christianity and Islam on the other hand, were dominated by those whose focus was on doctrine and rites, and who did not taken kindly to those who potentially challenged their doctrines with insights gleaned from personal praxis. Nevertheless, Jewish Kabbalists, Islamic Sufis, and Christian mystics have kept mysticism alive.

Forms of Jewish, Christian and Islamic mysticism were preserved throughout the centuries in various cults, whose existence was kept secret both to avoid persecution and because initiation into this knowledge was reserved for those who could appreciate it. Many, if not most of their ancient writings were either destroyed by the orthodox, or preserved in secrecy and lost to public view. Within the context of Judaism and Christianity, the discovery of the *Dead Sea Scrolls* and the *Nag Hammadi Library* have brought to light more of the ancient texts which reveal that the mystical element was lively both immediately preceding the lifetime of Jesus and for some time afterward. Contemporary scholars are also penetrating more deeply into the Judaic and Christian apocryphal writings, that is, non-canonical works. Historical research indicates that the mystical was strong from the very beginnings of Christianity and was only later overcome by an increasingly political and institutionalized church, together with a hierarchy vested in in their own brand of religious power.

The reading of scripture adopted herein follows a mystical tradition. Some of it is implicit in the canonical New Testament. Much more support is available from the non-canonical writings. However, since the present volume is not intended as a scholarly work, but simply as an introduction, we restrict ourselves to the familiar.

We must caution, however, that the intelligent appreciation of the New Testament, as with all ancient texts, requires the assistance of historical research and scholarship. It is very easy to fall into error by interpreting the records of another culture in terms of our own cultural bias. For example, in approaching the New Testament it is necessary to consider it in the context of the period which led up to it and the period in which it was actually composed and declared canonical – a span of some five hundred years, many forceful personalities, different sociological situations and various cultural inputs. Research shows incontrovertibly that the Gospels are neither biographies of Jesus nor accurate historical accounts, but rather are confessional in terms of the post-Easter *kerygma,* or apostolic preaching that the risen Jesus is the Christ, the Son of God.

In addition, the New Testament writings are not available to us in their original form. What we now possess has been redacted, that is, reworked in the process of transcription, so as to emphasize and even to interpolate developing theological positions. In this sense, we must remember that Jesus himself was not a "Christian" in our sense of the term.

Thus, we must be aware to cite scripture in support of a statement is not to adduce a proof but rather, an interpretation is being put on the scripture from a particular point or view. Scripture can be interpreted in a multitude of ways, depending on the level of intelligence, cultural orientation, historical awareness, and spiritual development of those who are reading it. For example, those who have deepened their experience through spiritual growth will interpret scripture differently from those who remain on the surface level of life.

As human beings, we all speak from our own level of intelligence, knowledge and spiritual evolution. We group ourselves together with those among whom we find agreement. For human beings in society, agreement is the ultimate criterion of truth and we tend to agree with those who are on our own level of experience and intelligence.

Thus, any statement concerning Christ's church that goes beyond describing its worldly manifestation as a religious institution is bound to fall short. For the church is made up of a variety of individuals, representing a spectrum of viewpoints. What is attempted here, for example, is simply to indicate the spiritual orientation of some of its members, who speak for themselves, at this time, and at this point in their spiritual development.

A traveler who seeks directions inquires from those who know the way. The experience of those who have gone before provides directions and landmarks on the spiritual path. They tell us both of the highways and the byways, the shortcuts and the blind alleys.

Ordination to the clergy initiates a person into the priestly way of life, whose proper task is performance of the sacramental rites. In some churches, the clergy have also assumed organizational responsibility. However, neither ordination to the clergy nor appointment to office can make a spiritual master.

A spiritual master is one who has trod the path successfully, with sufficient reflection on the process to be able to assist others in this goal. In order to take on such a role honestly and effectively, all who assume it must first become realized beings themselves, priests included.

In our view, the Christian religion consists of two fundamental aspects: sacramental rites and spiritual practice. The two go hand in hand to develop a person spiritually and to serve as a means of divine worship. While the clergy of the church perform the liturgical rites, spiritual direction is the role of those qualified to provide it.

While respecting the primacy of the person as the vehicle of spirituality, in agreement with the Protestant tradition, we recognize the value of structured practice, including the advantages of spiritual direction and sacramental grace. What is presented here is offered as a guide for those who wish to take counsel with fellow travelers on the spiritual journey.

No single expression, however rich and flexible, can be all things to all people. We welcome diversity in religion in general as well as in the Christian community, in order to provide alternatives for the many facets of culture and personality that God has created. We believe that our movement makes a distinctive contribution to the Christian perspective and provides an alternative that many people will find agreeable.

We respect the exoteric churches for spreading Christ's message widely. It is our position, however, that the exoteric is dependent on the esoteric, since a certain degree of culturing in spirituality is required before a person is capable of grasping even the rudiments of spiritual science. The exoteric is dependent on the esoteric, since a certain degree of culturing in spirituality is required before a person is capable of grasping even the rudiments of spiritual science.

Without the exoteric churches, Christianity would probably not have had the impact on the world that it has. The majority seeks shelter in the security of established doctrine, especially the notions of redemption and salvation through faith and good works.

Historically, it has been only a few in each generation who are willing to accept the mystery of divinity within as enough of a possibility to warrant the rigorous spiritual practice required to unfold it. The position which we are advancing emphasizes that spiritual knowledge is only gained within one's self through focused spiritual exercise. At this time, encouragingly, there seems to be a general awakening to spirituality and many are seeking to find divinity within. The Ascension Alliance provides a vehicle for such contemporary spiritual seekers that is both traditional and modern.

There is a Christian hermetic wisdom that has survived the inquisitions and persecution, and still exists in the present day. This knowledge has traditionally been kept "secret" for three major reasons: firstly, to publicly espouse unorthodox ways not only invites persecution, but it also needlessly confuses those who are immature in their appreciation and understanding. In the words of the Bhagavat Gita, "The wise do not confuse the ignorant." (Bhagavat Gita 3: 26). Secondly, the mysteries are not revealed openly, because it is possible to misuse power. Power can be used either for good, that is, unselfishly, or it can be used for ill, that is, for purely personal ends at the expense of others. Just as we do not let children play with matches, so too, the wise do not distribute tools of power to the spiritually immature. Exoteric knowledge and practices must first be utilized to prepare a person for the esoteric. One must first prove one's self before tools of power are communicated. Third, higher knowledge and practices are of a sacred nature and are reserved, not for those "worthy" of them, but rather, for those who can properly appreciate and utilize them. Unfortunately, the concept, "holy things for the holy," has kept many who could profit from these things isolated from them in the name of reverence. But who is the arbiter of who is "worthy"? Was not Jesus Himself criticized for associating with whores and thieves?

Reception of knowledge requires a probationary period, not as a proof of "worthiness," but rather, of readiness. When the learner is ready for the next step, the experienced teacher is perceptive enough to realize this, as well as competent enough to provide the proper stroke of instruction.

In some traditions, esoteric knowledge is given only after a long and arduous trial. Such systems are not well suited to the temperament to which our liberal, pluralistic, scientific, and democratic tradition has given rise.

Among others, pretense to knowledge is made, but no real substance is forthcoming. The well-meaning but unwary disciple is kept subservient to the leader and seniors, in a system that exists more for the accouterments of power it bestows on the hierarchy, than for the evolution it produces in the lowly.

In this regard, any system that claims to be exclusive in its knowledge or methodology is suspect, since there is no monopoly on wisdom. For wisdom is of the Spirit, an eternal and all pervasive reality that does not reveal itself in one form alone.

There are many who have wisdom, and there is no one who "has it all," to the exclusion of others. Everyone sees the world from his or her own perspective, and even the realized, although they may know the one identical Reality, frame it differently in their teaching and in their lives.

We all have many teachers, and our teachers also have their own teachers. As a matter of fact, everything in the universe is a potential teacher. Even the student teaches the teacher. As every teacher knows, teachers learn more from the students than students learn from the teacher. So teachers need students more than students need teachers.

Ultimately, however, there is only one Teacher – "the Christ" – or the God within. Books can testify to this, and earthly teachers can show the ways of approaching this truth, but only individuals can come to know themselves as they truly are – divine. Luckily for us, this Teacher also desperately needs us as His students. For His Spirit cannot rest until every particle of creation realizes its identity with Him.

MODERN AND TRADITIONAL

We embrace an ancient truth for a new age. We provide an intelligent alternative – traditional worship with free exploration of new ideas and techniques. Ours is both a traditional and a modern church. We maintain that eternal truth cloaks itself in garb appropriate to the age and that the form of religion should keep pace with human development.

In keeping with its contemporary stance, Ascension embraces a liberal philosophy. We welcome all to our congregations and erect no barriers or dogma or binding requirements of belief. We secure to our members full freedom of thought, belief, conscience and expression.

While conservatives may see this as inviting mayhem, we have faith that in the end, "Truth will win out." In our view, religion is not a matter of holding the correct beliefs; rather, it is aimed at attaining to divine wisdom. Those who "believe" do not know, since when one knows something, that person is no longer said to merely believe it. Beliefs, then, are but stepping stones to knowledge. Their role is "heuristic," that is, they serve as working principles, to be discarded when their purpose has been served.

According to the wise, spiritual wisdom is attained through self-study, and self-study requires the freedom to explore all possibilities. Under sincere scrutiny, the false drops off and the true emerges more and more into the light. What drops off as false are beliefs, for they are seen to be inadequate to their object, knowledge. Spiritual development requires the freedom to transcend limitation, even if the limitation is established doctrine. On the way, intelligent people may disagree and debate in the pursuit of greater knowledge, but mayhem is the province and mark of the ignorant.

Therefore, we do not flinch from acknowledging that freedom of conscience makes each person fully responsible for self-development; moreover, we fully recognize that freedom of thought and expression are essential to meet this responsibility. While admitting the importance of scripture and tradition as a guide, we encourage free interpretation of the scriptures, creeds, liturgy, and theology in the brightest light of contemporary knowledge.

Each of us must come to our own beliefs as a result of diligent application of both our innate intelligence and the measure of inspiration we receive. All seekers are encouraged to explore every resource relevant to spiritual development and personal growth, regardless of its source.

The recent history of our world is the story of rising global awareness, and consciousness of the one human family. The twenty-first century promises to be one of increasing unification as transportation and communications technology shrinks the distances, both physical and mental that separate us. The rising world economy is linking peoples and nations into a single planetary organism in a way that a political fiat could never accomplish as effectively.

A result of this unification is already being witnessed in the interaction of formerly disparate spiritual traditions in the minds of intelligent seekers. The visionary priest-scientist, Teilhard de Chardin, saw in this trend, which he traces from the inception of biological history, as God's plan for the evolution of planetary consciousness. We would like to think that we are now consciously participating in this plan.

While spiritual reality is eternal beyond space, time, and history, the Spirit unfolds itself in the world through Nature and humanity. Just as the Old Testament and the covenant it embodies was manifested historically and culturally in terms of the relatively tiny Hebrew nation over a certain limited period of time, so too the New Covenant was first announced to that same small nation in the context of a different historical epoch, with very different cultural conditions. Outside its own internal records, which are regrettably scanty, the dawning of Christianity and its initial period of development went virtually unnoticed by history.

The Christian church as it has unfolded subsequently has developed under the enormously diverse influence of many cultures and historical factors, not the least of which is humanity's growing awareness of global unity. What began as an isolated cultural phenomenon has assumed world historical importance.

The religious challenge of our time is to create the bridge from limited cultural conceptions to a grand synthesis that is capable of embracing the eternal spiritual truth which is a truth for all peoples and all times. Rather than continue a cultural bias, we propose to unite not only the best in the Christian tradition, but the best in all traditions. By the best, we mean the eternal, living, element that can be found everywhere as a living expression of the Spirit.

The Trappist author, Thomas Merton, sought this common ground through his travels among spiritual people of the East. His later writings are an indication of the coming direction in religious ecumenism, which seeks to uncover the underlying Spirit beneath diverse cultural manifestations.

We do not shrink from embracing the Spirit of God wherever it has cloaked itself in earthly form. The Ascension Alliance welcomes this cross-fertilization and invites all to investigate the rich spiritual traditions both of other Christian denominations and of non-Christian religions and wisdom traditions.

There being only one Supreme Reality which manifests its providence through the action of the Holy Spirit, all spiritual paths are ways of the Spirit, to the Spirit, by the Spirit. The same may also be said for ancient mystical traditions, as well as modern wisdom. Therefore, we find no conflict either in participating with other organizations or adopting ideas and practices from other spiritual, religious, and metaphysical traditions.

We look forward with great expectation for the *Third Millennium* to be an unprecedented era of spiritual growth, as all branches of human knowledge converge holistically. This is a particularly exhilarating time to be present on the scene, consciously participating in the unfolding of unity in diversity on a grand scale.

OUR LIBERAL TRADITION

The present-day Ascension movement views itself as liberated from a law that had become crystallized and which emphasized the letter over the spirit. We see ourselves as an alternative to Christian backsliding into the legalistic rigidity that Jesus had roundly condemned.

Since its beginning in the earthly ministry of Jesus, some two millennia ago, the Christian church has undergone a series of transformations that have altered it significantly. Over time, historical and cultural influences, such as the installation of Christianity as the official religion of the Roman Empire and the marriage of Christian doctrine with Greek philosophy, radically altered the Church as a temporal institution. The institutional church became infected to the degree that the Protestant Reformation was necessary to purify it of its excrescence. The reformers were well intentioned in returning responsibility for spiritual development to the individual person. However, their subsequent rejection of the sacramental rites, along with apostolic succession that perpetuates sacramental efficacy, was a most radical departure. The present-day The Ascension Alliance proposes to overcome these difficulties by providing a fresh alternative that the Counter Reformation did not.

Ascension as a Church and religious jurisdiction is neither Roman Catholic, Eastern Orthodox, nor Protestant. It recognizes that all these churches and the rest of Christianity have much that is valuable for religious life today. We seek to unite the best of these traditions. We follow the traditions of the Catholic and Orthodox rites with respect to ritual and liturgical practice, perpetuating the efficacy of the sacraments and the validity of orders by preserving the apostolic succession. But we believe that in order to make it alive today, we must express the impulses and insights of the historic Church in creative rites and open praxis. We respect the great work already accomplished in maintaining the authenticity of Christ's teaching through scholarship, councils, theology, and so forth. We honor this tradition by entering into a "conversation" with it, learning from it, and listening to new insight from Spirit.

With respect to ritual and liturgical practice, we take a somewhat conservative position. We adhere strictly to the essentials of liturgical form and the necessity of a valid apostolic succession. However, with respect to other matters, such as scriptural interpretation and theology, we take a more "hands off" stance.

From the liberal Protestant tradition, we derive our commitment to the freedom of the individual person with respect to both thought and conscience. Therefore, we make no demands on the individual with respect to belief or performance.

This does not imply that we in any way abdicate the teaching role of the Church. While we reserve ultimate choice to the individual we teach that diligent study and intelligent deliberation are prerequisite to an informed conscience, freedom of choice implies responsibility and one of our first responsibilities as intelligent beings is to be reasonably informed.

On the other hand, to ask people to profess views to which they do not fully subscribe is to invite insincerity. We agree with Saint Thomas Aquinas that the moral law requires that, after due deliberation and prayerful reflection, we follow the dictates of conscience unswervingly. If a person does this, he is accounted as without blame, even if it turns out that the judgment was in error.

We accept the scriptures and traditions of the Church as guides but not dogma, to be appreciated in the light of scholarly research. We reject the view that one party to a controversy has the right to decide the debate by fiat. Instead, we trust Spirit to resolve the controversy to the good of all if we but pray together over the matter, and we persist in rigorous inquiry and polite dialogue until the resolution becomes obvious to all concerned.

If we hold to any dogma, it is that each one of us is fully responsible before God for the use we make of our intelligence, free will, and inborn abilities. If there is truth in the notion that God created man "in His image and likeness," then what is necessary for full spiritual development is within each and every human being. "The kingdom of heaven is within you," recalls the words of the psalmist, "Be still and know I am God" (Psalms 46:10; Luke 17:21). The external forms of religion should serve to enliven this inner expression of divinity, which is the human birthright, rather than to obscure it.

Christians believe that the Christian church exists as a visible manifestation of invisible grace, whereby God provides explicit guidance to man both through the inspiration of the Holy Spirit and by means of sacramental rites. Christ's church exists for the individual as an external manifestation of what is already an inborn reality in every human being.

God does not impose religion on man; religion is an explicit expression of the implicit Law regulating all life, ordering it back to its Infinite Source. The one true religion is ever present in the heart of man as the inspiration of the Holy Spirit. The various churches are but means of awakening man to what is already eternally present within the human heart.

In addition to providing for divine worship, a primary mission of Ascension is to foster spiritual science and to administer the sacraments as visible signs of an outpouring of divine Grace upon the world, thereby enlivening the spiritual consciousness implicit in everyone. At the same time, we maintain that the scriptures and traditions of the church are rich in inspiration regarding faith and morals. We recommend this rich tradition as a guide in fulfilling the responsibilities that intelligence and freedom of choice entail.

While the Ascension organization leaves individuals free to follow the dictates of their conscience, we counsel that all have the responsibility to inform themselves intelligently and to deliberate sincerely regarding principles and choices. We recommend that they consult our Christian scriptures and traditions, as well as the other wisdom traditions of the world, and that they interpret them in terms of the best thinking of our age.

In this sense then, Ascension has definite spiritual principles and Christian guidelines which it recommends to its members for their consideration; yet, we leave assent to the individual. While no particular belief is required for membership, acceptance of a path of spirituality in the Christ, as one perceives it in his or her heart, is understood as our common bond.

We take our common faith to be the foundation of our association. For us, faith is trust in God's unconditional love for us. We understand faith as fellowship with the Christ, God incarnate, and with each other in the life of the Spirit, rather than as commonality of belief. We trust in the inspiration of the Holy Spirit to lead all sincere seekers to the goal to which they earnestly desire. "Ask and you shall receive; seek and you shall find; knock and it shall be opened unto you" (Luke 11:10).

SPIRITUAL SCIENCE

Because we take a liberal stance with respect to doctrine and canon, you should not therefore assume we have no fixed principles and think that truth is relative and arbitrary. We hold that spiritual truth is an eternal reality and that it makes itself known in the hearts of sincere men and women everywhere.

This truth is also manifest in creation as the patterned workings of the Spirit that comprise the laws of spiritual science. These laws are obvious to all with eyes that can see and ears that can hear. In the words, "If your eye be single," many feel that Jesus is referring to the third eye, the eye of spiritual sight (Matthew 6:22; Luke 11:34).

The third eye is a metaphysical faculty, similar to physical sight, but nonmaterial and operating on subtler planes. Clairvoyance and clairaudience are sensory manifestations of this phenomenon and developed intuition is its intellectual manifestation. Full development of the third eye makes the adept omniscient.

The scriptures, mythologies and mystical pronouncements of the saints and sages are all revelations of spiritual science, expressed in language and symbolism that inadequately captures its essence, due to the fact that conceptual thought and language are linear, while spiritual science is holistic. As the great German philosopher G. W. F. Hegel admonishes, "The truth is the whole."

For this reason, spiritual science is knowable only in a holistic state of awareness, which is gained through spiritual practice and achieved at the level of adeptship. Prior to adeptship, we see "only through a glass darkly." After realization is gained. "then we shall see face to face" (1 Corinthians 13:12).

The spiritual aspirant begins by transcending the animal nature, which takes sensory information as the ultimate justification of truth, regards sense pleasure as real happiness, and mistakes the empirical ego as the true self. To ordinary consciousness, justification of hypotheses is limited to empirical verification, sense gratification is confused with real happiness, and the spiritual person is overshadowed by the individual personality.

While empirical verification is entirely appropriate as a methodology to use at the physical level to suppose that the methodology of the physical sciences is the paradigm for true knowledge is a tragic error. For it puts beyond the pale of human knowledge the vast realm of wisdom which includes virtually everything that is really worth knowing.

What is really worth knowing is not the realm of fact, which is physical but of value, but that is metaphysical. For we desire what we value and what we desire most is fulfillment. Moreover, we are impelled by nature to seek fulfillment incessantly. Physical reality is not sufficient to satisfy spiritual being for long, because the material world is always changing. We eat only to become hungry again. Sense gratification is always temporary. Human beings can never find fulfillment through their animal nature.

The realm of true value is the eternal and unchanging. Therefore, the Absolute alone is capable of providing real and abiding fulfillment. This is the subject of spiritual science. It is sung of by the poets, hankered after by the philosophers and theologians, pointed to by the prophets, and testified to by the mystics. Each aspirant must discover it within on his or her own spiritual journey.

Spiritual science cannot be gleaned from external means, such as books. It is only available on the inner planes, within the depths of one's own being where the link is discovered to the greater Being. Its fruit is variously called gnosis, mystical experience, Divine Union, Brahmavidya, Veda, becoming a Buddha, Tao, and other things, each expressing a different view of the same ultimate Truth.

The word "spiritual" means both 'holistic' and 'openness to transcendence.' Spiritual science is founded on a methodology for transcending ordinary human states to true wisdom knowledge of one's own true nature, the God within. In this sense, spiritual science is a "spiritual alchemy," so to speak, in which the gross is sublimated and refined, transmuted and transformed into the subtle. Ordinary human awareness, its own true nature forgotten, is progressively transmuted and transformed into the God within.

The methodology of spiritual transformation is called a process of "refinement," because nothing is added to produce holistic awareness, but rather, the dross of ignorance is simply purified out and removed, leaving what was hidden under the film of forgetfulness on the surface of consciousness.

Thus the fruit of spiritual science is not available to ordinary awareness, which is characteristic of the limited ego, studied by contemporary empirical psychology. Metaphysical truth dawns only in more expanded levels of consciousness. It is available in its totality only to those who have attained holistic awareness.

To those whose eye is single, this truth is everywhere obvious. This one truth, called "the perennial philosophy," is found repeated by the saints and sages, poets and wise people throughout history and is recorded in the sacred books, mythologies and literature of all cultures. It is in our own Judaeo-Christian scriptures and in our liturgy. It is the basis of the principles we hold dear and live by. It is unmistakably in every atom of creation. There is nowhere it is not.

To those who have attained holistic awareness, Yahweh is truly I AM. Jesus' purported statements, "I and the Father are one," and "I AM [is] the way, the truth and the life," may be understood to be this knowledge that in the fully realized being, all is one (John 10:30; 14:6). This can be seen in the same mystery proclaimed by Krishna, "The spiritual adept sees Me in all things and sees everything in Me. Indeed, the adept sees Me everywhere. For the one who sees Me everywhere and sees everything in Me, I AM [is] never lost to him, nor is he ever unknown to Me" (Bhagavad Gita 6:29-30). In both cases, Jesus' use of "I" and Krishna's use of "Me" can be interpreted to refer not to the physical manifestation of either Jesus or Krishna, but rather to the holistic awareness of which each is the paradigm and embodiment.

Thus, our commitment to freedom of belief and conscience stems not from any apprehension that truth either does not exist or cannot be known. On the contrary, The Ascension Alliance is mystical. Mystics hold from experience that divinity reveals itself within to the sincere, and that Christians are called to a personal relationship with "Christ" as the highest *in* us – an eternal reality waiting to be "remembered," as Plato describes it.

We hold that religious ritual is concerned with the distribution of spiritual power in the world in a way that is perceivable to the subtle sensibility. Similarly, following ethical precepts also involves a noticeable building of character over time, while ignoring or contravening moral principles, results in a diminution which is obvious to anyone who is at all sensitive.

Our liberal stance stems from our conviction that the truth dawns naturally in the hearts of the sincere in its own time, and cannot be forced on the unwilling. We leave everyone free with respect to belief and conscience, secure that the truth will be realized quickly if people are left to their own devices, instead of being stuffed with doctrine, so they don't have to grow, or, worse, being bludgeoned into submission. The result of such prodding is the parroting of catechism and mere physical presence at services that is of little avail with respect to the practice of spiritual science.

We stand ever ready as a beacon for those who want to achieve a deeper appreciation of spirituality. Our clergy serve as ministers of sacred rites and initiations, helping channel spiritual energy into the world. We regard our sacred tradition as most precious and we perform its ministrations faithfully, in accord with ancient traditions. However, we regard ourselves as more than mere keepers of convention.

PURPOSE

Jesus Christ instituted His Church to perpetuate His public ministry by personally training the apostles to continue what he had begun. The apostles were instructed both before and after the Resurrection and they were spiritually vivified in a special way at the time of the descent of the Holy Spirit upon them. We presume they realized the immense value of what they had received, and handed along to their successors the essentials of what Jesus had taught them. From the New Testament and the traditions of the early church, we can gather that the external mission of the nascent Church consisted of divine worship through the sacraments, together with preaching the Gospel and the advice of the elders. We are reasonably secure that the efficacy of the sacramental rites has been authentically preserved through the apostolic succession of orders and that the scriptures contain the thrust of the public teaching of Jesus during his lifetime. Beyond this, however, controversy rages concerning historical details and correct interpretation.

Moreover, it is far from clear what aspects of tradition stem from Jesus and the apostles and what was added. For example, the New Testament implies that Jesus spoke to the people in parables, but later taught the disciples their inner meaning (Matthew 13:36). However, in the Gospels and Epistles, there exists scant record of the details of Jesus' esoteric teaching and we must assume that any record we have of it is preserved in apocryphal writings, historical references, and the early tradition of the Christian church.

The Church Father Clement, for example, mentions that the Gospel of Mark contained an esoteric portion which was deleted for public consumption. This section has unfortunately been lost. Lacking either an exact formulation of Christ's esoteric teaching, and even many of the early records themselves, we can now only speculate on what Jesus may have imparted privately.

Even with respect to His public ministry, we are in the dark with respect to a great deal even concerning the sayings of Jesus. Standards of scholarship are far different now than they were hundreds and thousands of years ago. Early writers, for example, in their zeal to establish the truth of their points, attributed later innovations to earlier notables, to include even Jesus and the apostles. While interpolations are easier to locate and remove, skillful redactions that subtly rework the sense of a passage are more difficult to detect and restore.

Moreover, the scriptures are far from obvious in their interpretation, as the centuries of subsequent controversy go to show. In addition, tradition is difficult to unravel, a great deal of it having accrued from diverse sources of varying value. Furthermore, an entire theology and philosophy has sprouted from the fertile field of speculation, watered by alien sources and cultural bias. And when Christianity became the official religion of the Roman Empire, the church took on a political nature that deeply affected its subsequent development. One noteworthy result was that the former emphasis on freedom from oppressive views gave way to the necessity for assent to orthodoxy.

For such reasons, we do not take the purpose of the church to be magisterial in the traditional sense of becoming authoritarian and dogmatic. We feel that we can best fulfill Christ's purpose by dispensing the sacraments, perpetuating the apostolic succession of orders, providing guidance into a more considered appreciation of Christian scripture and tradition, and fostering spiritual science through practice, rather than by taking yet another stance with respect to orthodoxy.

Accordingly, instead of taking a position regarding acceptable interpretation of Holy Scripture, particular application of Christian morality in people's lives, or doctrinal orthodoxy, we recommend that scripture and tradition, theology and philosophy, be used as tools, along with all other relevant materials, in coming to an intelligent appreciation of our Christ's message. While we take a metaphysical stance, we do not insist that anyone adopt it.

We hold that the essence of faith is not intellectual assent or doctrinal belief, but rather trust in the Lord. The faith that Jesus recommends to us is epitomized by the psalmist, "The Lord is my shepherd; I shall not want" (Psalm 23; Luke 12: 22-34). Faith involves placing one's trust in the Spirit as an all powerful evolutionary force guiding each of us to perfection, as well as the Creation as a whole. Faith is reliance on this invisible power of the Spirit working within us to return ourselves to God. This is the faith by which we are born again.

While baptism of the body is accomplished by water, baptism of the Spirit is worked by faith. Just as water nourishes all life, especially in the minds of a semi-desert people like the ancient Palestinian Jews, so too faith replenishes and renews life in the Spirit for those liberated from fear. Through faith, we can truthfully say, "O Death, where is thy sting?"

While we are born again into the Spirit through the sacrament of Baptism, whereby we publicly declare our conversion and establish our intent to live always in faith, we must continuously be born again in faith through our ongoing commitment to the life of the Spirit.

Through faith, we renounce the view that we are limited beings, functioning as stimulus response mechanisms, like other animals. Through faith, we recognize ourselves as essentially unlimited through our free will and intelligence, which faculties permit us to share in the creative nature of God. Our hearts are ever open to the inspiration of the Spirit to uplift and enlighten us.

To be born again, in this sense, is to renounce all considerations of being a victim of circumstances, to trust in the love of God to work the best in all situations, and at all times to use our free choice and creative intelligence to unfold to our maximum potential as spiritual beings. For history demonstrates time and again that when men and women ally themselves with the Spirit virtually nothing is impossible for them. And this is the word of the Gospel (Luke 17:6).

Our purposes fall into at least two categories: first, the mystical and the metaphysical; secondly, the sacramental. With respect to the first, Christian scripture and tradition, doctrine and creeds, the sacraments and rites of the church, all contain many levels of meaning and truth, literal, symbolic, and spiritual. We act as guides through these levels, helping seekers on the way to becoming spiritual adepts through spiritual exercise and practice.

Spiritual life involves coming to know God, first through the intellectual conviction of divinity within and without; then, through faith in God's unconditional love for us as children; next, through a personal relationship with the divine form through spiritual practice and divine grace; finally, through divine union in spiritual experience. In recognizing this course of spiritual advancement, we acknowledge our affinity with the saints, the holy ones, and the mystics of all ages, cultures, and religions.

With respect to a second aspect of its mission, Ascension clergy administer the traditional sacramental rites as means of visibly distributing Christ's love in the world, acting as a channel for spiritual power. We regard the sacraments as initiations into deeper levels of truth and portals to more subtle planes of existence. Through sacramental initiation, contact with subtler dimensions is established, leading the aspirant on to ever higher levels of spiritual unfoldment.

Through the Holy Eucharist, the Christ is directly available. Through Baptism and Confirmation, special channels for the Holy Spirit are opened. Through Reconciliation and Holy Unction, Christ's healing power is poured out through the ministrations of His healing angels, healing not only physical aberrations, but everything standing in the way of wholeness. In Holy Matrimony, and in each of the steps of Holy Orders, the soul takes on more and more the quality of a channel through which the Christ can flow into the world.

The Primacy of the Spiritual and Mystical

Our orientation is mystical insofar as we emphasize the primacy of spiritual experience, rather than a commitment to a certain set of beliefs, or adherence to a particular theological or philosophical doctrine. We acknowledge that the greatest advancement in the search for spiritual truth is made by those who discover that divinity resides within. In our view, the essence of the Gospel is, "The kingdom of heaven is within you," echoing the words of the psalmist, "Be still and know I AM God" (Psalms 46:10; Luke 17:21).

The question then becomes, how to gain access to the kingdom? The traditional answer of Judaism was to follow the Law, and Jesus was in agreement. He pointed out, however, that the essence of the Law is love (Matthew 22:35-40). John testifies that "God is love" (1 John 416). If God is love, then to the degree that we truly love, we experience divine union. It is through our love that we come to a real and abiding knowledge of God. For Christians, love is spiritual knowledge par excellence. Our goal is to love, even as we are loved by God. The Christian path is the way of love (1 John 4:7-21).

We hold that external forms of worship, such as the sacramental rites, are aids to a contemplative way life, not substitutes for it. External forms of worship find their value in the internal transformations they serve to accomplish, in conjunction with spiritual practice. Along with liturgical worship, we recommend a life of prayer, meditation, and contemplation as leading to a life of spiritual illumination.

The reading of scripture, both Christian and non-Christian, and about the living examples of the saints and sages of all cultures, is also a recommended spiritual practice. In our view, this meditative reading is valuable due to the uplifting effect of associating our consciousness with those of the Holy one's. This subtle effect is even more significant than the intellectual insights which may be gained. Placing one's mind in contact with the minds of the saints and the sages aligns us with the Spirit in them.

This is not to ignore the value of service and good works, which are methods of active meditation. Service and good works are the manifestation of an interior state of being which sees everyone and everything as united in Our Lord Christ.

Moreover, prayer itself is defined as a lifelong giving up of our own minds and hearts to God. We are admonished to pray unceasingly (1 Thessalonians 5:17). True faith, the attitude that everything about life is spiritual and that God is the One in Whom we live, move and have our being, is the ongoing prayer of the heart that makes all of our doings an active form of meditation, and all daily life a spiritual exercise.

ESOTERIC

Out orientation is also esoteric, as opposed to exoteric. Recognizing that the scriptures and liturgy are symbols of a deeper reality, we seek to draw back the veil of ignorance which hides the true spiritual import of religious symbolism. While we appreciate the literal and historical dimension of Christianity in the life of Jesus of Nazareth, with which exoteric traditions seem most concerned, we emphasize the spiritual import of these teachings over the historical particulars that may have surrounded them. Although the Hebrew Scriptures contain valuable records of the history of the Jewish people, we are more concerned with the spiritual import of their symbology. Scientific discoveries, for example, have made it clear to intelligent people that the creation myth of Genesis is not meant to be taken as a literal description of historical fact, but rather as an allegory with a spiritual meaning, which is complementary to a scientific understanding of how historical events have unfolded. Few today, other than the diehards, are willing to defend Biblical "creationism," for example, as a viable scientific theory challenging what scientists have come to call "normal science," so universal is its acceptance.

For us, it is not a matter of either science or religion, but of both/and. One can be a good scientist, and at the same time be a mystic and accomplished metaphysician. Whereas the scientist theorizes about such things as energy and information, the mystic discovers the experience of existence and intelligence as an essential part of holistic awareness.

From this perspective, the Biblical accounts are not important so much for their literal and historical aspects, as they are for their metaphorical, allegorical and, anagogical (spiritual) import. The scriptures of all cultures, for the esotericist, are records left by the enlightened sages, which tell the story of the unfolding of holistic awareness. Their language is not literal, but "mythological." It conveys itself in a form that has exoteric appeal, hence, it is regarded as valuable, worthy to be transmitted from generation to generations, even by those who do not understand its deeper meaning, resting there where it can await new waves of spiritual seekers.

The myth of the Garden of Eden and the Fall, upon which the doctrine of original sin is based, is a story that most children of western countries are familiar with. Yet, it contains the deepest of spiritual insights. Far from describing historical facts literally, according to the esotericist, the myth discloses the process by which the Spirit descends into matter. The ensuing duality between knower and known is the result of Spirit's identification with a body, which is also the basis of spiritual ignorance, according to those we account as wise. Spiritual ignorance, the absence of holistic awareness, is the illusion experienced by the knowing subject that he or she is separate from the known object. The result of this duality is *fragmented awareness,* the erroneous belief that "I am separate and distinct from everyone and everything else in the universe." In the esoteric understanding of the Christian *mythos*, the Christ, representing holistic awareness, liberates those who gain mystical unity with "Him" from the spiritual ignorance of fragmented awareness. We exist in Him just as He exists in the Creator.

From this perspective, the history of exoteric Judaism and Christianity is the story of overcoming the guilt of sin, both "original sin," i.e., genetic sin, and our own sins, where "sin" is taken to mean *a spiritual debt incurred due to moral wrongdoing*. The esoteric view is that sin is a symbol of spiritual ignorance, and that Our Lord Christ comes not so much externally to redeem humanity from moral deficiency, as to liberate it internally of the illusion of duality and multiplicity that veils our essential unity in God.

In our view, the Christian message is one of happiness and joy, not of suffering and self-deprecation, as it has so often been represented in scriptural interpretation, theological doctrine, liturgical expression, and sacred art, especially since the time of Augustine. Born again through our faith and trust in the Lord, we rejoice in the assurance of our salvation. We interpret redemption and salvation as liberation, that is, the progressive drawing back of the veil of spiritual ignorance until we no longer see "through a glass, darkly, but then face to face"(1 Corinthians 13:12).

Moreover, the *Dead Sea Scrolls* show that the Essene community was one of esoteric spiritual practices, and mystical bent. Their view was, very likely, a significant influence on both John the Baptist and Jesus. This suggests that the esoteric tradition concerning the early life of Jesus is simplistic. Jesus could have been trained to become a spiritual adept and mystic master from an early age, and in all probability was at least cognizant of the contemporary mystical teachings, perhaps even those of Egypt and the East. Little enough is actually known about the historical Jesus anyway, and the esoteric nature of such things would make them even more likely to be suppressed than ordinary facts.

Paul, whose theology was so influential in the development of Christianity had also been a disciple in a mystical school of the Pharisees. The authors of the Johannine writings were likewise steeped in a mystical tradition. The Nag Hammadi find reveals that much of the non-canonical literature of early Christianity is unabashedly gnostic.

It is indisputable that many of those who have followed the spiritual path, whether Christians or mystics of other traditions, have discovered through spiritual practice what they take to be transcendental experience. This spiritual dimension is the basis of the perennial philosophy which reveals itself as mysticism and metaphysics in all epochs extending from prehistory to the present, and in all climes from the Himalayas to the New World. We find it unreasonable to divorce the Christian message from this perennial wisdom, especially in favor of what seems to us to be superstition akin to that found in virtually all naive forms of religion.

Exoteric religions stand opposed to this perennial philosophy in their emphasis on the institution at the expense of the person, on authoritarian dogma in place of spiritual experience, and on otherworldly salvation instead of liberation from ignorance in this life. Exoteric philosophies and psychologies conflict with the perennial in their confusion of the eternal person with the temporal personality. The exoteric sciences stand opposed to the esoteric, owing to their emphasis on verification by the senses as the ultimate criterion of truth, at the expense of spiritual experience.

Thus, we avail ourselves of the value of the sacramental tradition, as well as of the knowledge of spiritual science. We offer a combination of advantages that is relatively unique in the world today.

We extend our invitation to all who are free thinkers, aspiring mystics, metaphysical seekers and sacramental enthusiasts, to join with us in spiritual fellowship and divine worship. The need is also great for clergy to perpetuate our tradition and to make it more widely available as the Spirit works Its ways through people of good will in the Third Millennium.

Under the leavening influence of the Spirit in human life, we expect this time to be one of Heaven descending to Earth, and Earth ascending to Heaven. We look forward to the Second Coming of Christ, not so much as an apocalyptic phenomenon, but as a transformation in the personal lives of each and everyone of us, and in the transformation of the world into one of peace and love.

The Ascension movement endeavors to provide an opportunity to participate in the resurgence of Christian mysticism, which leaves the individual free to determine truth for himself or herself through a process of Self-unfoldment. We combine personal responsibility for growth with traditional sacramental rites. Our orders are readily available to qualified candidates who feel called to ordained ministry and we are among the few rites that permit clergy to marry if they choose, and that open Holy Orders to women.

The adopted liturgies of the Ascension organization have been designed to communicate this esoteric understanding by removing reference to sin and its forgiveness, since the connotation these words have accumulated have become emotionally "loaded," especially for those who have been exposed to more exoteric Christian interpretations of them. Instead, we emphasize the overcoming of spiritual ignorance, first by adopting an attitude of faith as trust in God's love for us; secondly, by opening our hearts to the grace that God freely offers us through the sacraments; thirdly, by developing spiritual discipline in our lives, to include prayer, meditation, and service.

METAPHYSICAL

Metaphysics is an aspect of spiritual science, based upon experiential knowledge of the subtler planes of existence, something which is acquired through mystical experience. Mystical experience is intuitive – a higher level of perception. Therefore, the basis of good metaphysics is not deductive reasoning, which is hypothetical and only as strong as the assumptions on which it is founded. Nor is it inductive reasoning, which is empirically based, and therefore subject to the limitations of the physical senses.

The difficulty with this kind of knowledge, relying as it does on subjectively experienced mystical experience, lies in the availability of adequate criteria for judging its truth. While deductive reasoning can display its logical pedigree and inductive reasoning its empirical merit, metaphysics makes its appeal to intuition, a notoriously fallible faculty. Nor are all "metaphysicians" above dissimulation, a caution to be wary in a field where verification is not available to those who lack holistic awareness themselves, i.e., the very people most likely to be taken in.

Therefore, we recommend metaphysical study primarily through the process of spiritual growth in which holistic awareness is its own immediate criterion, according to mystics and seers, and only secondarily through intellectual inquiry, where an adequate criterion is lacking.

Through spiritual development, metaphysical knowledge spontaneously unfolds in a way that is experiential. The testimony of those who have gone before then becomes a yardstick for appreciating our own increasing intuition and higher perception. This testimony also plays the role of a guide, both by suggesting where we might fruitfully look for results as we begin to develop spiritually, and also by recommending methodologies which have shown themselves to be successful.

The Ascension organization is mystically oriented insofar as we maintain that real knowledge of God is available while we are yet in this world, through the process of spiritual development. While this is not an item of dogma with us, it does indicate a fundamental metaphysical orientation.

There are two metaphysical positions that find themselves in conflict in Christianity. The exoteric one has been widely held as orthodox because its proponents achieved a position of power in the early church, declaring other competing view, the esoteric position, as heretical often punishable by death. The esoteric position was forced to "go underground," sometimes perpetuated in secret societies. The esoteric has resurfaced publicly in the atmosphere of religious tolerance and freedom which has emerged in the modern era.

One exoteric position is based on a literal interpretation of *Genesis,* to the effect that God created the world and remains ever separate from it. Therefore, human beings are helpless to bridge the gap and are completely dependent on divine grace for salvation. This attitude found its epitome in the Calvinistic doctrine that only a few people, i.e., themselves, had been chosen to receive the grace necessary for salvation.

A more esoteric position suggests that creation emanates from God like rays of light that emanate from the sun. Creation is only seemingly separate from God for those who are unaware of the totality for those who hold this view. For the aspirant, God is transcendent. For the adept, God is immanent. From an esoteric perspective, the process of spiritual development is the regaining of holistic awareness, culminating in the discovery that the source of one's being is the One, the All in All. The goal of spiritual development, then, is not salvation from the damning effects of sin, but rather liberation from the bonds of ignorance, such liberation constituting spiritual enlightenment.

According to the Gospels, Jesus refers to God as "Abba," which is usually translated as "father," but is more familiar and colloquial, and is more accurately translated as "daddy." The emphasis is on the closeness of an intimate personal relationship. To the ancients, the child was separate from the father physically, but not spiritually. The child was not thought of as created by the father, but rather as emanated from him, possessing his characteristics and His "spirit," so to speak.

In our view, by calling God, *Abba,* Jesus was emphasizing the essential spiritual connection running through all existence, just as the spirit of the father is communicated to the children. Jesus may have claimed that He was consciously aware of this connection when He said, "I and the Father are one" (John 10:30). The Gospel also calls us to this degree of oneness, this perfection, "Be perfect, even as the Father is perfect" (Matthew 5:48). The apostle Paul emphasizes this same spiritual connection of the All in the All, by acknowledging God as "Him in who we live, move, and have our being." (Acts 17:28).

We call attention to scriptural references not by way of proof but rather to indicate our experience in reading it. The proof we hold, lies in the direct mystical experience.

Mystics and spiritual adepts of all ages and cultures have reported spiritual development as the expansion of consciousness to all-inclusive proportions. The finite is discovered not to be separate from the Infinite, but rather an illusion of duality created within the Infinite by itself, out of its own creative energy, or *Maya* as the Hindus would say. The process of spiritual evolution has been described by adepts as "God playing hide-and-seek with Himself," and enlightenment as a "waking up," or "remembering one's true nature."

We view Jesus as not only a mystic, par excellence, but also as a master metaphysician, and a spiritual adept of the highest order. We question whether it is reasonable to attribute to Jesus, on the basis of a literal reading of the Gospel accounts alone, an exoteric metaphysical view that seems to conflict so profoundly with the lofty spiritual experiences of so many accomplished mystics – Christians, Hasidim, Kabbalists, yogis, arahats, Sufis, Taoist sages, naguals, and shamans.

We point to the saints and mystics of all religions and cultures, who testify that in addition to the visible material level there are many subtler layers of existence; that the spiritual world is vast and powerful; that the mighty Intelligences that inhabit the spiritual world are in the service of God and at the aid of man; that the ultimate reality of all the worlds is the Absolute, that mystical experience is genuine, and that real knowledge of God is achievable in this earthly life.

In the state of Unity, at the apex of spiritual illumination, the distinction between immanent and transcendent, matter and spirits, and subject and object is overcome. To this exalted state, all are called and all are chosen. This we hold is the true meaning of redemption and salvation. Our Lord Christ is called the Redeemer, as the source of our spiritual liberation from ignorance, and our awakening to the truth of our essential nature.

Our views are in consonance with those of many other metaphysically oriented traditions and organizations. All are welcome to pursue their studies as they wish and to form associations as they choose.

A wide spectrum of metaphysical options exists and the neophyte should examine the field before settling on a particular viewpoint. While it is true that there is a "perennial philosophy" as an esoteric, metaphysical, and mystical undercurrent running through human culture, there is wide divergence within it. Instead of seeking for the ultimate metaphysical system, many aspirants choose to glean what they deem most valuable from many sources, proving the insights they have already experienced in their ongoing quest to develop spiritual excellence.

The wise caution, however, is that spiritual development is not achieved by "dabblers," those who experiment with many paths and techniques, never committing to a way that has proven successful to others in producing mystical realization. While we encourage study and experimentation to a degree, we admonish that there is the danger that an uncircumspect eclecticism may produce only spiritual dilettantes. For this reason, the wise aspirant prefers a guide who has already trod the path successfully.

GOD

The very essence of religion as a human activity is divine worship, whose highest purpose is the attainment of union with the divine. This presupposes a notion of the divine. Since our concern here is simply to present an introduction to the the orientation of the Ascension Alliance, this is not the place to enter into a philosophical or theological disquisition into the nature of divinity. However, since participation in Ascension involves a religious way of life, we must consider the question in sufficient depth for our present undertaking.

"God" is a term, that is, a linguistic sign, which signifies by means of the mental construct it calls to mind. For example, our English word "God" is related etymologically to "good," or value. The Vedic concept, "Brahman," means great, a notion also attributed by the Chinese to the Tao (Tao Te Ching XXXIV). Whatever the word chosen to signify the Supreme, the term relates to the reality it purports to signify, through the medium of a mental construct, which is dependent on human consciousness, and which includes the influence of all our human limitations.

Our mental constructs are limited by the mode of knowing, of human awareness. Ordinary human awareness is restricted in its ability to fashion a suitable mental construct to represent the reality of the divine because the divine is by definition metaphysically transcendental. For example, God is not a being of the same order as other beings; for the Creator is the source and ground of being. As Saint

Thomas Aquinas put it, "We can know *that* God is, but not *what* God is." That is to say, intellectually we can know that God exists, but our intellects cannot comprehend the divine nature nor can our languages capture it. Mystics may report experiences of divine union, but these reports cannot themselves duplicate the experience for another. Thus, mystical experience is said to be ineffable.

Theologians and philosophers, those who have deeply examined how thought and language function to represent the metaphysical, are generally in agreement that there are only two ways that we can speak of the divine. The first is the *via negativa,* or the way of negating all limitation, and the second is by means of analogy, for example, the way of super-eminent attribution, that is, of attributing positive qualities to God to the superlative degree.

The *via negativa* simply denies all limitation to God. As the Upanishads succinctly put it, "not this, not that." For the Taoist, "Those who know, do not speak, those who speak do not know" (Tao Ye Chin XLVI). Buddhists simply refrain from any attempt to signify the Transcendent. Or, as we night ourselves say, God is infinite, that is, not finite.

As Aquinas noted, even when we say things that seem to attribute real attributes to God, they are disguised negations. For example, when we say that God is one we are denying that multiplicity and divisibility apply to God. When we say that God is Spirit, we are saying that God is transcendental, that is, beyond the pale of limited existence and therefore beyond our ordinary mode of knowing, bound as it is by precepts and concepts.

The other way of speaking of the divine is through analogy, by attributing to God supereminent attributes. That is to say, we idealize aspects of our knowledge and experience and attribute these to God.

When we call God the Creator, for example, we are attributing the abilities and function of an artist, an engineer, or an architect, even though God's nature greatly exceeds anything we can imagine or conceive of, not only in scope and magnitude but also in degree. The divine nature is an altogether different order of being. God is not another being in the ordinary sense, but rather the one "in whom we live, move and have our being" (Acts 17:28). Properly speaking, we cannot say that God either exists or does not exist, for our linguistic concept of existence is bound up in limitation. To get around this difficulty, we show super-eminent attribution by capitalizing terms referring to God to show that they are being used in a special way.

The advantage of analogy by super-eminent attribution is that we feel uplifted in attributing to God the highest value. The disadvantage is that we tend to anthropomorphize. That is to say, we create a mental construct of God in our own image and likeness, often ending up worshiping an idol, so to speak, of our own fancy.

The real difficulty in this is that idols all have feet of clay. Our theological constructs, no matter how clever and elaborate, become riddled with contradiction to the degree that they attempt to contain an infinite dimension in a limited space. The result is that people get fed up with the posturing and declare that "God is dead," whereas the truth is the anthropomorphic idea of God as stillborn from the start.

Judaism and Islam in their essence, present the divine as strictly ineffable and beyond symbolic representation, although both of these religions contain an enormous anthropomorphic lore in their exoteric aspects. Metaphysical religions such as Vedanta, Buddhism and Taoism try to avoid the "problem of God" by emphasizing the via negativa and focusing on spiritual methodology, that is, ways of effecting transcendence. All this being said, esoteric Hinduism, Buddhism and Taoism are replete with anthropomorphic conceptions of their own, involving a pantheon of deities, various Buddhas and Taoist immortals.

In Christianity, of course, we focus our devotion on Our Lord Christ in the person of Jesus, while we assuage our intellects with the "mysteries" of the Blessed Trinity and the Incarnation, to dissipate our "cloud of unknowing." Curious anthropomorphic lore has grown up in Christianity just as it has in other religions.

This general tendency to anthropomorphize in religion is an indication that ordinary consciousness needs a focal point for devotion. A transcendental Supreme is too abstract for the majority of seekers.

On the other hand, the saints, sages and mystics of all religions and wisdom traditions testify from experience that while God is transcendent in the sense of being beyond all limitation and beyond ordinary modes of knowing, the Transcendent is also Immanent as the very substance of all that is. Spiritual practice is capable of revealing to the aspirant the divinity within, as the source and ground of our being.

Where the human mind falls short, the human spirit picks up. In fact, divine union in the yogic tradition of Patanjali is said to occur in a state of consciousness beyond all mental activity. God is known in silence. In the words of the Hebrew scripture, "Be still and know that I AM (God)" (Psalms 46:10).

The sages have unanimously advised spiritual methodology, the way of transcendence, as the way to give real meaning to the concept of God. In the words of the philosopher Emmanuel Kant "concepts without experience are empty."

The concept of God based on anthropomorphism, that is, attributing human characteristics to Him or Her, is inadequate and misleading. The concept of God attained intellectually through the way of negation is empty and unsatisfying. To grow into a real knowledge of the divine, spiritual methodology is a prerequisite.

The essence of spiritual methodology involves an unfolding awareness of the immanent divinity within; therefore, spiritual methodology is fundamentally experiential. The admonition of the Delphic Oracle, "Know thy Self," is echoed in the Vedic and Buddhist injunction to transcend ordinary experience through self-realization. The Hebrew, "Be still and know that I AM (God)," presages Christ's message, "The kingdom of heaven is within you" (Psalms 46 10; Luke 17:21).

The Lord reveals Himself to Moses as I AM (Exodus 3:13-15). This is the basis of spiritual science, for it indicates that the essence of divinity is to be conceived of by us using an analogy based upon our own awareness. "I" indicates subjectivity and "to be" may indicate either predication or existence. As Descartes noticed, "I" implies the "am" of existence "I think; therefore, I am." To be a subject is to be conscious, and to be conscious, if only of one's self is to exist and to know that one exists.

God is quintessentially I AM, because God is both the ground of all existence and the eternal knower of Himself. Everything which exists, exists in God. In knowing the Divine Nature, God knows all possibility and actuality eternally, beyond space, time and change.

We can conceive of creation taking place through God's knowing the divine nature fully, throughout the range of possibility, from infinite to finite. In God, since knowing and being are one, when the finite range of possibility is known, the finite comes to be and, being finite, "forgets" that it is God. Yet, error cannot persist in the presence of truth, so the finite contains within itself the dynamic principle of evolution that leads it back to the infinite.

In this model of evolutionary development, human beings are initially born into finitude to rediscover their infinity. Spiritual science reveals that the way to this discovery is through the I AM. By turning the awareness within and transcending ordinary experience through spiritual practice, we discover our true nature to be I AM or pure consciousness, that is, consciousness knowing nothing but itself and all in itself

This knowledge is unitary and completely fulfilling, for the desire of the knower is fully satisfied in the totality of knowledge of the Self; there is no further to go. Since this experience alone is completely fulfilling, our implicit desire for it drives us in its pursuit, until we recognize that worldly pleasures, being finite, can never really satisfy us. The whispering of the Spirit in our hearts, calling us home to unity with God within, I AM, is responsible for the divine discontent which keeps us ever on the evolutionary march.

Yet, in speaking this way of "Self" and "I AM," we must hearken to the Buddhists admonition against using terminology, such as "Self" and "I AM" for the Buddha nature, i.e., fully awakened enlightenment. As adherents to the via negativa, they wisely caution against using any words to signify a reality that completely transcends the ordinary human experience, whence all conventional language derives its meaning. In this view, capitalizing words to indicate technical spiritual meanings is more likely to lead to mystification than to true mysticism.

ONE TRUE PATH?

We assert that we are a limb of the one, holy, universal way created as a seed by God, Who planted it in the human spirit that it might sprout as a guide to truth. The Holy Spirit ever acts through the hearts of sincere seekers, regardless of creed or culture, to bring them to the knowledge and love of God. This and no other is the one, true, and ancient religion through which God binds creation back to its Source. All religions are manifestations of the one unmanifest Truth that unfolds itself within.

The work of the great psychologist, Carl Gustaf Jung, brought to light archetypes of the collective unconscious as fundamental structures of human intelligence. The basic themes common to cultural phenomena, including religious myths, are traceable to these archetypes. They reveal that it is not by accident or chance that the mythologies of various cultures resemble each other, or that religions are concerned with typical subjects and deal in similar concepts. Cultural expression, including religious life, unfolds from the inside out, so to speak, just as does personal spiritual experience.

Far from implying that spirituality is merely a figment of the imagination, and religion a cultural phenomenon, these archetypes give us a glimpse into the seed idea from which God created the human spirit. Just as the laws of nature are hidden behind the phenomena they regulate, so too, the workings of the Spirit that guide human destiny are hidden from view. And, just as laws of nature have been discovered by science, so too, the inner workings of the Spirit are disclosed to conscious awareness by spiritual practice.

For this reason, the saints of all religions and the sages of all cultures have advised looking for ultimate answers within. Hinduism, Buddhism and Taoism are noted for the subjective orientation of their spiritual practices, while the Delphic Oracle's "Know thy Self," and the Old Testament's "Be still and know I AM God," echo Christ's words, "The kingdom of heaven is within you" (Psalms 46:10; Luke 17:21).

CHRISTIAN UNITY

Two great schisms have divided the Christian religious community. The first great schism occurred when the western Catholic and eastern Orthodox factions disagreed, ostensibly over how to express the nature of Christ in the official creed. One faction insisted upon the description, "homo ousia," or "of the same substance" with the Father, and the other faction held out for *"homoi ousia,"* that is, "of like substance" with the Father. Thus, Christendom was divided over an iota.

Many other more minor breaks have occurred over the span of Christian history. However, after the Christian Church gained imperial status, deviations from the dominant position were condemned as heresies and their adherents disposed of before an actual schism could perpetuate itself widely. For centuries an aura of orthodoxy and appearance of unity was maintained by force.

The second great schism occurred when the internal corruption of the Roman Church, together with a growing nationalism in Europe, made the Protestant Reformation possible. Once again, a proliferation of sects occurred, actually returning Christianity to a state much closer to the earliest days, when there were many different ideologies that called themselves Christian.

There are now an estimated 20,000 denominations of Christianity, each holding differences significant enough to call for separate congregations. Some decry this proliferation as contrary to Christ's intention to create a single church.

In our view, all Christians are already united in Christ, regardless of external appearances, and doctrinal or liturgical phenomena. There is only one unmanifest Christian Church which appropriately expresses itself in many forms due to the richness of its message and the diversity of human types.

Rather than an external political unification, a unified doctrine, a single creed, an accepted interpretation of scripture, or a standard liturgy, what unites Christianity is the unmanifest spiritual power that grounds it, and without which it could not have remained vibrant for two millennia. Christ's power is the basis of Christian unity. "Where two or three are gathered for My sake, I AM [is] there with them" (Matthew 18:20).

We love all Christians in spiritual fellowship, as instructed by the Master, keeping in mind His admonition, "You will be known as My followers by the love you show for one another" (John 13:35). We honor and respect all Christian sects in their differences, as well as in their similarities, for we recognize that the richness of Christ's message, together with the broad diversity of human personality, has produced a single garden from flowers of many types.

CHRISTOLOGY

Most Christians regard Jesus Christ not only as the latest and greatest of the Hebrew prophets, but also as the very incarnation of God in human form. Some of a more esoteric persuasion see Jesus as the vehicle for Our Lord Christ in this age. In this view, while Jesus came to realize His divinity, Our Lord Christ did not come to a realization of his unity with the Divine through the process of spiritual evolution, unlike the realized yogis and saints, and the higher orders of beings such as the Angels and other Holy one's, but rather, possesses it eternally.

However one conceives of the relationship of Jesus and Christ, Christ is believed to exist eternally as God the Son, the Second Person of the Blessed Trinity, in unity with God the Father and God the Holy Spirit, one God in three Divine Persons (John 8:58). Precisely what this means is a matter of dispute among many Christian sects, as well as between those who adhere to exoteric and esoteric interpretations.

Just as the existence of the one true God Who made a covenant with Israel is fundamental to Judaism, so too, the mysteries of the Blessed Trinity and the Incarnation are basic to Christianity. As mysteries, they are ineffable; however, symbolically they embody basic truths of spiritual science which must be plumbed within oneself. The mystical position is that these symbols are not unraveled by intellectual inquiry, but rather by spiritual exercise.

Nevertheless, the mystical Christian may fruitfully conceive of these mysteries by analogy. One familiar with Oriental mysticism and philosophy may interpret the Trinity as the unity of Self-knower, Self-knowledge and Self-knowing in Self-knowingness, the state of spiritual enlightenment which is the goal of spiritual practice.

The knower of the Self is the progenitor, the knowledge of the Self is the only begotten, and the knowing of the Self is the activity (breath, spirit) uniting them all, being identical with the Self. Spiritual enlightenment is the experiential transcending of experiences, experience and experiencing, each of which alone is partial and fragmented. The adept discovers that the divine within is the unity of knower, known and knowing in Self-knowingness.

Saint Thomas Aquinas also held that the Blessed Trinity can be conceived of analogously from what we know of our own consciousness. For, if we are made in God's image and likeness and if God is not material then our consciousness is that which is most spiritual in us and must reflect the divine nature more closely than the body. Reflection on our own experience reveals that consciousness is reflective, that is, both exists and knows that it exists. In addition, human awareness is also intelligent and feeling.

Saint Thomas Aquinas develops the analogy quite ingeniously. God the Father, being pure Consciousness, knows Himself in Himself, through Himself and by Himself, as self-existent. His knowledge of Himself proceeds from Himself alone and is identical with Him. God's knowledge of Himself that is, of His own Nature, is the Son. "I and the Father are one" (John 10:30). The Son proceeds from the Father as pure Intelligence, in an eternal process of self-referral. "In the beginning was the Word, and the Word was with God and the Word was God" (John 1:1).

Consciousness also has an affective component. The self-referential knowledge of God is accompanied by supreme fulfillment. To put it poetically, the love that proceeds from the Father's knowing the Son and the Son's knowing the Father, being identical with this process of reciprocal knowledge occurring eternally within itself is also identical with God. The Holy Spirit is this pure Love (1 John 4:7-16).

While we locate the masculine principle in the almighty Father as pure existence and pure Power, the Holy Spirit as pure Love reflects the essence of the feminine principle, the Great Mother. Jesus as the Son embodies the masculinity of the Father, the Holy Lady Mary personifies the Divine Mother.

That the early Hebrew prophets considered God androgynous finds support in *Genesis*. There the word expressing the Creator is the Hebrew, "elohim," a plural form. The text reads, "And Elohim said, 'Let us make humanity in our image, after our likeness....' So Elohim created humanity in his own image, in the image of Elohim he created them, male and female he created them" (Genesis 1:26-27).

This finds its parallel, for example, in the Vedic conception of Shiva and His consort, Shakti, Mother Divine, the womb of the Universe. From the mystical perspective of the realized, Shiva is pure consciousness and Shakti is the nature of this consciousness that is open to itself through self-knowledge. Through God's knowing His nature, it becomes Mother Nature. Similarly, the Taoist sage discovers within the silence of Tao, the dynamical interaction of yang with yin, creative with receptive, heaven with earth, male with female, from which proceeds "the ten thousand things."

We also recognize the similarity of the Incarnation with the concept of the Avatar, as in Hinduism. Just as Our Lord Christ is the eternally omnipresent, omniscient and omnipotent, despite the temporal Incarnation, so too Krishna is the representation of the Formless One in form. Instead of being embarrassed by the "coincidence" and attempting to explain it away, we recognize and appreciate incarnation of deity as a fundamental archetype of the human spirit implanted by the Creator as an essential element of true religion, signifying the eternal reality of divinity within.

Now that science has penetrated so many of the secrets of the Universe, we have come to realize that in all likelihood other planets support intelligent life, perhaps much like ours. Presumably, God has provided for them also, but it is unlikely that they call any such incarnations provided them, "Jesus of Nazareth." Why should not the Second Person of the Blessed Trinity incarnate on separate occasions in circumstances appropriate to different cultural conditions. Just as Hindus have no difficulty recognizing their conception of the avatar in the popular conception of Jesus Christ as Divine Incarnation, so too intelligent and open-minded Christians have no difficulty recognizing their conception of incarnation in Bhagavan Krishna.

As a Christian church, The Ascension Alliance acknowledges the spiritual leadership of Our Lord Christ, Who is its founder, living head, and eternal High Priest. As a Catholic church, our clergy perform the sacramental rites that are traditionally accepted as having been instituted by Jesus Christ during His earthly mission. Furthermore, The Ascension Alliance recognizes the scriptures and traditions of Christ's church as guides for spiritual life and religious practice.

For us, the proof of Christ's leadership lies in the spiritual power we derive from our association with Him through our own spiritual practices, the liturgy, and the sacraments. What one intellectually believes about Christ is not as important as the relationship one cultivates with Him through one's worship.

In our fellowship, we allow for differences in opinion concerning Christology. The traditional position is that Jesus Christ was both God and man from the moment of the Immaculate Conception. The metaphysical view is that Jesus of Nazareth was a high adept who made his earthly vehicle available to the Lord Christ at the time of the baptism by John at the beginning of His public ministry. A third view is that Jesus was indeed the last of the great Hebrew prophets, whom the Christ Spirit overshadowed but never actually identified with in material form. Other views are possible, of course.

For example, on the hypothesis that Jesus was influenced by the Essenes, or traveled in Egypt and the East, some find it spiritually conducive to consider Jesus in the role of Master, the task of whose disciples is to unite their limited minds progressively with the master's holistic awareness, whereas Our Lord Christ is viewed by them as transcending the limitation of Jesus' form and personality. Others find it more appropriate to follow the traditional belief, namely that Jesus is the Christ, the Son of God, from the moment of his conception by the Holy Spirit of the Virgin Mary.

The question is not which version is "true," but rather which one is most conducive to a person's spiritual growth. In fact, over the course of a person's spiritual journey it would not be unusual for one's Christology to change considerably, with deeper and more expanded experience.

The view that one adopts regarding Christology is immaterial to spiritual development as long as one is sincere in the pursuit of perfection. Just as the sun shines on the righteous and the unregenerate alike, so too the power of Christ's love is available to all true seekers regardless of doctrinal orthodoxy. God searches our hearts, rather than inventorying our intellectual beliefs.

This is not to say that anyone is encouraged to believe anything that one fancies. Religions, as sociological phenomena, have been filled with superstition, especially in their popular forms. We do not seek to perpetuate this unfortunate inclination on the part of the credulous.

Nevertheless, we recognize that in the past there has been the tendency to confuse *unshakable conviction* with *incontrovertible fact*. The "faithful" have often been all too quick to condemn as heresy anything that challenges their religious world view. As a result, the exoteric view has been complemented by an esoteric one that perpetuated itself as an underground movement, for fear of reprisal, and even persecution. In our pluralistic society, however, there is no longer need to continue this sham. People should be free to espouse publicly what they truly hold. History shows that when ideas can freely confront each other in an atmosphere of free expression and pursuit of truth then knowledge grows and superstition wanes.

While Rudolf Bultmann suggests that virtually nothing is known concerning the actual facts in the life of the historical Jesus of Nazareth, more recent scholarship paints a different picture. Marcus Borg and others have now studied the words of Jesus intensely and extensively. Scholars associated with the Jesus Seminar have explored what they believe are the authentic words of Jesus of Nazareth. Also, through interfaith discussions and a study of cultures, we may now be able to deduce much of what the life of Jesus was actually like. This study includes an exploration of the context of the times, geographical location, historical context, etc. Old Testament scholars (and New Testament scholars as well) curiously enough, until the last fifty years, did not consult their counterpart Jewish colleagues, for whom the study of the Torah/Tanakh is like life itself. Only recently has the Jewish context been included in the study of the life of Jesus in New Testament scholarship! When Bultmann wrote these words, this new conversation had not yet taken place.

We are not quite left to our own devices, then, when it comes to settling upon a view that is conducive to our own inclinations and purposes. There are a number of other options, in addition to the traditional accounts, that offer to guide us. Cayce, Levi, Prophet, and other "new age" oracles provide a series of options based on intuitive sources. The *Dead Sea Scrolls* and the *Nag Hammadi Library* present historical material which may be read as challenging the traditional views. In fact, there has probably been more written about Jesus of Nazareth than any other mythic-historical figure.

We recommend balancing investigations into the more flamboyant theories with reference to the studies of historians and Biblical scholars. These are trained professionals who scrutinize the available material from an unbiased, scientific perspective, through the lens of vast knowledge of the field, and a rigorous methodology. Their findings are important factors in overcoming undue credulity.

In fact, there is an emerging field, called "Jesus research," which is delving into the new information provided by archaeological discoveries and advanced textual methodologies, in order to establish the most conclusive data. James H. Charlesworth's *Jesus Within Judaism: New Light From Exciting Archaeological Discoveries* is an excellent introduction to this field, and Professor Charlesworth provides an annotated bibliography of the most recent research, including appraisal of the non-scholarly positions.

Also to be recommended as an introduction to the relevance of the *Nag Hammadi Library* is Elaine Pagels' *The Gnostic Gospels*. Professor Pagels' work demonstrates that the conception of Jesus in the early churches was richer than what emerged as the traditional position – a view which dominated only after the earlier diversity had been relegated to the realm of "heresy" by the triumphant conservative faction.

We do not officially sanction any particular view of Christology. We are aware that this is a controversial field which is just now being examined in a new light, given the pluralistic and scientific bent of our times. We encourage open study and debate concerning even the most fundamental issues regarding our Christian heritage, and leave it ultimately to the individual to establish anew that personal relationship with the Christ which is the mark of the sincere Christian.

APOSTOLIC

Our Church holds "apostolic succession," passed on by the apostles to all present-day bishops, through successive generations of bishops, in accord with ancient custom. In this way, we are connected with the personal ministry of Jesus. The Ascension Alliance traces the validity of its orders to the consecration of Evodius as the very first Patriarch of Antioch by the apostle Peter, in an unbroken succession of consecrations, traceable through many lines. A summary of this succession follows.

Christian tradition maintains that the twelve apostles were commissioned by Jesus as his special delegates, as is well known from the New Testament account. One of the twelve, Judas Iscariot, betrayed

Jesus and took his own life. The other apostles received their consecration by the Holy Spirit, as Jesus had promised, on the original Pentecost. This consolidated the power that Jesus had delegated to them, and empowered them to actually carry out the mission they had been given by Jesus.

The evidence of their rebirth in the Spirit is attested to not only by their charisma, such as the ability to speak in tongues, but also by their fearlessness in the face of danger. Whereas they had been afraid of meeting the same fate as their master and had hidden themselves away prior to the descent of the Holy Spirit upon them, after Pentecost they went forth to proclaim the Good News openly and boldly (Acts 1-4:32).

It is also reported that Peter felt that the defection of Judas had left a hole, or lacuna, in their ranks and asked the brethren to select a replacement. When the assembly chose Matthias, he was also numbered among the apostles, setting the precedent for apostolic succession (Acts 1: 15-26). As the church grew, more ministers were required and the apostles requested the brethren to select assistants for them. The apostles prayed over those chosen, and laid hands upon them to consecrate their ministry, establishing the basis for future transmittal of Holy Orders (Acts 6:1-6).

Since the earliest times, these things have been repeated in the church, perpetuating the tradition of episcopal succession and the rite of Holy Orders. All present day Catholic and Orthodox bishops trace their lineage to these same beginnings.

In this way, our Church traces its temporal beginnings to the city of Antioch, in Syria, in 38 A.D. Saint Paul had ventured to Antioch to preach the

Gospel, where it was received by a large number of Gentiles (Acts 11:19-25;13:1-52). Previously, the church had been largely confined to Palestine, where it was centered in Jerusalem and consisted almost exclusively of Messianic Jews. With the rise of a community in Antioch, a momentous question was posed: Should the Gentiles, who were being received in accordance with the Master's instruction: "Go and teach all nations," be subject to the Jewish Law (Acts 15:1-5)?

The matter came to a head when Peter traveled to Antioch and was rebuked by Paul for his failure to stand by the principle that the Gentiles were not subject to the Jewish Law, the following of which was taken as the sign of observance of the Old Covenant (Gal. 2:11-21). Rather than maintaining the community as a Messianic sect of Judaism, the apostles decided that non-Jewish members were not subject to Jewish Law, thereby creating a new autonomous body fully governed by the principles of a New Covenant, the sign of whose observance was following Christ (Acts 15:6-35). Thus, in Antioch Christianity became an independent religion, as scripture reports, "it was in Antioch that the disciples were first called Christians" (Acts 11:26). After the destruction of Jerusalem in 70 A.D., this Church became became our Mother Church. Our present connection with the ancient lineage of the apostles is through Archbishop Herman Adrian Spruit, who was formerly a Methodist minister and an associate of Ernest Holmes, author of *The Science of Mind*, in the Church of Religious Science. Dr. Spruit was ordained a priest in April 1956 by Bishop Charles Hampton, Regionary Bishop of the Liberal Catholic Church for America and Canada. On June 22, 1957, Spruit was consecrated a bishop by Bishop Hampton, along with co-consecrators, Bishops Wadle and Marshall of the American Catholic Church. On June 26, 1960, Archbishop Paulus Aphostratus and Bishop Michael Strange elevated Bishop Spruit to the status of archbishop.

The consecration by Bishop Charles Hampton connected Spruit with the Dutch Old Catholic succession, which first came into being in 1724, when a Roman Catholic bishop consecrated the leader of a small band of Dutch Catholics in overwhelmingly Calvinist Holland. This succession was brought to England through the consecration of Arnold Harris Matthew at the Old Catholic Cathedral of St. Gertrude's, in 1908, in Utrecht, the Netherlands. Later Matthew, who consecrated James Ingall Wedgwood, founder of the Liberal Catholic Church, of which Charles Hampton was to become the Regionary Bishop for North America.

Archbishop Spruit credited Bishop Hampton with being an especially bright light, which still serves as a beacon for the present day Independent Catholic movement, and strongly reflecting Hampton's liberal and esoteric bent. Hampton's Liberal Catholic Church, although true to its Dutch and English roots, was watered in American pluralism, and emphasized intellectual freedom and personal responsibility. It also embraced esotericism, which was derived originally from the connection of its founders with the Theosophical Society. Bishop Hampton bequeathed these influences to succeeding generations of spiritual pilgrims.

The connection of our organization to the ancient Syrian Church of Antioch is through the Syro-

Malabar succession, conveyed to Bishop Spruit by his co-consecrator, Bishop Lowell Paul Wadle. The Syro-Malabar succession was brought to North America by Archbishop Joseph René Villate, who was consecrated as the first Old Catholic Archbishop of North America by Archbishop Francis Xavier Alvarez in the Ceylon in 1892, pursuant to a Bull issued by His Holiness Moran Mar Ignatius Peter, Patriarch of Antioch and all the East, of the (Jocobite) Syrian Orthodox Church of Antioch. The Bull authorized Villate's consecration and named him metropolitan for North America.

Archbishop Villate conveyed his succession to Bishop F. E. J. Lloyd, who, in turn, conveyed it to Archbishop Gregory Lines, who then passed it to Archbishop Robert Raleigh.

On June 27, 1965, Archbishop Robert Raleigh and Archbishop Spruit imposed hands on each other in a specific ceremony, just for the purpose, of uniting their successions, and, in the event of the demise or incapacitation of Archbishop Raleigh, to set aside Archbishop Spruit as as his successor. Archbishop Spruit succeeded to this position on the passing of Archbishop Raleigh in 1970, changing the name of Raleigh's jurisdiction to the Catholic Apostolic Church of Antioch - Malabar Rite, to reflect the Antiochian roots.

We mention only the most prominent lines of apostolic succession, but many more lines are included, in the order of seventeen, in fact. A publication, "Our 17 Lines of Apostolic Succession" is available to interested persons from the Catholic Apostolic Church of Antioch.

Archbishop Spruit's association with Bishop Charles Hampton and his commitment to both liberalism and esotericism gave him a different approach to Catholicism than had been taken by the traditional Antiochian, Syrian Orthodox, church. In the words of our *Statement of Principles*, "in its doctrinal position we hold that there is a body of Truth, which is common to all the leading religious systems of the world, and which cannot be claimed as the exclusive possession of any one of them. In this respect, we differ from the majority of churches in Christendom."

To establish the uniqueness of the "Church of Antioch," as it had come to be known, Archbishop Spruit established his church as a patriarchate, and took the title of Adrian VIII. Upon the passing of Bishop Anthony J. Aneed, who left in his last will and testament his own claim to the North America Patriarchate of the Greek Melchites to Archbishop Spruit (the Greek Melchite Church is one of three *uniat* patriarchates of Antioch in communion with Rome, the other two being the Marionites, *Patriarchatus Anfiochemis Syro-Maronitarum,* and the *Syrian Patriarchatus Antiochenus Syrorum).*

The *Statement of Principles* of the Catholic Apostolic Church of Antioch holds that it is "a constituent part of the One, Holy, Catholic, Apostolic, Church, which is truly One because the One Life of the Christ animates and sustains it through the Sacraments which He instituted and blessed." Likewise, we embrace that Truth for ourselves.

In 2006 Alan R. Kemp was consecrated a bishop in the Catholic Apostolic Church of Antioch by Archbishop Richard Gundrey, Bishop Paul Clemens, and Bishop Kera Hamilton. Upon Archbishop Gundrey's retirement, Kemp briefly served as Interim Presiding Bishop of that organization. He soon left the Church of Antioch over concerns about its new leadership, direction, and philosophy. Later, he transformed his own organization from a mission community of the Church of Antioch into the Ascension Alliance, an independent, free, Church inspired by the "Independent Catholic," "Emerging Church," and "Jewish Renewal" movements.

Sacraments and Sacramentals

The saints and holy one's of all religions and cultures testify to the efficacy of religious rites to distribute spiritual power. Virtually all religious systems practice some form of "ceremonial magic," as it were, in which the performance of certain rites is oriented to the accomplishment of definite results, sometimes of a purely spiritual nature, but often of a material nature also, under the influence of the spiritual.

The conditions for proper performance traditionally involve both *competence* and *authority* on the part of the priesthood. That is to say, the priest should be competent to perform the rite with respect to ritual and rubric, and should also be authorized to do so by proper authority, usually through an appropriate initiation, or series of initiations.

Shamanistic systems are replete with such phenomena. In addition, the great religions also practiced a form of "sacred magic," as in the sacrifices performed by the Levitical priesthood of the ancient Hebrews and the Vedic *yagyas* performed by the Brahman priesthood.

While the conservative element may not like to think of the sacraments in these terms, a Christian "ceremonial sacred magic" is performed by an initiated priesthood. The rites are highly regulated through the liturgy, and the priesthood is required to be duly authorized through the proper initiation rites, known as Holy Orders, which, in turn, must be performed under the authority of the apostolic succession.

The Christian ceremonial is embodied in the sacraments and sacramentals, the performance of which by competent and authorized persons is claimed to have definite results on both the spiritual and material planes. The necessary and sufficient conditions for sacramental efficacy are, in fact, competence and authority. First, the priest must be duly ordained by a bishop whose own consecration is valid in terms of the apostolic succession. Then, if only the proper ritual and rubrics are used (proper form – i.e., an approved liturgy performed in accordance with the canon) and the actual intent to perform the sacrament, is sacramental efficacy assured, according to the accepted tradition.

Moreover, since the sacraments and sacramentals are primarily ordered to transforming the base into the refined, and even to transmuting the very nature of the material into the spiritual, they may be conceived of as a form of "spiritual alchemy," so to speak. Just as the bread and wine are changed into the Body and Blood of Christ at the Transubstantiation, so too is the materially oriented individual transformed into the spiritual through the sacramental grace of the Holy Spirit.

We feel that it is important to emphasize the "magical" quality of the sacraments and sacramentals, because in our scientific age, religious ceremonial is liable to be viewed by the "scientific" as a sort of "living fossil." Even many of the faithful consider the sacred rites to be either merely symbolic or completely mysterious. However, clairvoyants report that the sacraments and sacramentals are not merely curious ceremonial performances. C. W. Leadbeater, late Presiding Bishop of the Liberal Catholic Church, in his book, *The Science of the Sacraments,* has meticulously detailed his clairvoyant observations, and Geoffery Hodson, a Liberal Catholic priest, also contributed to this clairvoyant research. Others with refined perception, many of whom have not published their observations, affirm that observable subtle phenomena take place during the performance of these rites.

While we are not "Leadbeaterites," we do maintain that the sacraments and sacramentals are not merely ceremonial performances, nor are they only symbolic, nor are they so purely spiritual in their result as to be completely mysterious to us. We would also add that a person does not need fully developed refined perception, in order to be able to appreciate the subtle effects of the sacraments.

To those who begin to practice "noticing," a definite transformation occurs when one receives the Eucharist for example, as well as during the Service of Healing, both of which are especially powerful in their effects upon the person receiving them. Reception of Holy Orders also brings a noticeable infusion of upliftment, and many who receive Baptism still have charismatic experiences, recalling those reported in the early Christian literature.

The Christian church administers seven sacraments, along with other liturgical rites, such as the Benediction of the Most Blessed Sacrament. The sacraments are visible channels of invisible divine grace, freely communicated by God both for the spiritual perfection of individuals and for the upliftment of the world. The sacraments are instruments of spiritual power given to us by God both for our sanctification and as initiations into ever deeper realms of the spiritual.

In addition to the seven traditional sacraments, tradition has conveyed through the ages many sacramentals, such as the Sign of the Cross, Benediction of the Most Blessed Sacrament, the Divine Office, and so forth, for the further proliferation of spiritual upliftment and divine grace. While the sacramentals do not carry the same distinction as the sacraments, they are nevertheless powerful rituals in their own right. Even something as simple as the sign of the cross made over oneself has an effect perceptible to the sensitive.

The Ascension Alliance recognizes the same seven sacraments as other Catholic and Orthodox rites, namely, Baptism, Confirmation, Holy Eucharist, Absolution (also called "Reconciliation" and "Penance"), Holy Unction, Holy Matrimony, and Holy Orders. As a guarantee of the continuing efficacy in their administration, the Ascension organization endeavors to ensure that its liturgies conform to all the essentials and that the orders of its clergy proceed from the apostolic succession of the episcopacy.

Through the sacraments, particularly the Holy Eucharist, also known as Holy Communion and the Sacrifice of the Mass, Christ maintains tangible contact with His people and confers His strength and blessings upon them.

HOLY EUCHARIST

The Ascension organization concurs with all Catholic and Orthodox rites that the sacrament of the Holy Eucharist effects a real and not a merely symbolic communion with Christ. Sacrifice has from the most ancient times been regarded as a most potent rite. It is a recognition that the Lord, as the Source and Goal, is the giver and taker of life (Lev. 17:1-14). In the Hebrew Scripture, Yahweh Himself is reported as directly decreeing the sacrificial rites, which since the destruction of the Temple in 70 A.D. have ceased. The sacrifice of the Mass is virtually the last remaining sacrificial rite still performed. Nor is it merely symbolic; for we take the Body and Blood of Jesus Christ to be actually present as it was at the Last Supper and temporal Crucifixion.

In the celebration of the Holy Eucharist, the Offertory corresponds to the offering of the oblation to the deity in sacrificial ritual; the Consecration to the immolation of the sacrificial victim; and, the Communion to the partaking of the oblation by the priests and institutors of the rite. The other portions of the Mass have their significance in erecting the spiritual temple and its altar at which the sacrifice is performed.

Spiritual sacrifice is not exclusive to the Eucharistic rite. Rig Veda, for example, records the primeval and, indeed, eternal sacrifice in which the one Self of all is at once the sacrificer, the sacrificed, and also the sacrifice (Rig Veda X: 81.82). The act of sacrifice is the portrayal of one of the deepest mysteries of spiritual science, namely, how the many proceed from the One and how multiplicity returns to its unitary Source without ever leaving it. The Holy Eucharist is an initiation into this most profound mystery, which is unveiled only in the depths of personal spiritual experience.

All reverent people are welcome to receive the Holy Eucharist at our altars, whether they are members of our church or not. For we believe that all who sincerely desire to partake of this unparalleled channel of grace should have the opportunity to do so. The effect of receiving this sacrament can only help to uplift. Those in need of improvement should not be denied this most valuable aid, so we communicate all who reverently approach our altars.

ABSOLUTION

The sacrament of Absolution derives directly from Christ's bestowing the power of forgiveness on the apostles (John 20: 21-23). Recalling that we pray, "Forgive us our trespasses as we forgive those who trespass against us," we hold that the efficacy of Absolution is in proportion to the sincerity and resolve of those who partake of it.

The sacrament of Absolution is an initiation into the mystery of self transcendence. Forgiveness implies prior offense and grounds for resentment. At less expanded levels of awareness, in which the dichotomy between self and other is experienced as obvious, taking offense and feeling resentment are ordinary occurrences. Here, forgiveness involves overcoming the limitations of egoistic concern.

Through the process of forgiveness, coupled with other spiritual practices, one comes to realize that forgiveness is the psychological antidote for taking offense and feeling resentment. If no offense is taken, no resentment is felt and no forgiveness is necessary. At advanced levels of experience, the realized fully identify with the one Self of all and find that it is impossible for the Self to take offense against itself. The question of forgiveness dissolves with the dissolution of the grounds for offense and resentment.

This reveals that the conventional interpretation of original sin and the necessity for a divine redeemer is the result of religious anthropomorphism, since only an anthropomorphic deity could be resentful. When the symbolic nature of the Fall is understood as the fall of the original wholeness into fragmentary awareness, then we can appreciate how, through the loss of this view, a theology of sin and atonement eclipsed spiritual science and veiled the knowledge of how ignorance is overcome through divine wisdom.

For spiritual science, the concepts of original sin and redemption play an important part in the mystery of self-transcendence, since their inner meaning is bound up in the loss of wholeness and the spiritual journey back to it. Human beings, by taking on individuality, are born in ignorance of their divine birthright and they reawaken to wholeness only through the process of spiritual development.

"Sin," in this view, is not seen as an offense against an almighty being whose sense of justice requires recompense, even at the expense of eternal damnation of its creations. Rather, this view seems to many to be unworthy of an intelligent concept of deity, and certainly contradicts the very nature of God as love that is put forward by Christianity as one of its major contributions to religious thought.

Because of its unfortunate connotations, we prefer not to use the concept of sin, either in our thought or in our liturgy. We do not deny, however, that unrighteous thinking and conduct is spiritually detrimental. Unrighteous thinking and conduct is that which is essentially egocentric, for what is essentially egocentric separates us from holistic awareness. Human beings are said symbolically to be "guilty of original sin," a condition "that condemns them to eternal damnation," because we are born into a state of fragmented awareness, in which we will persist until our unregenerate nature is changed into a state of wholeness through spiritual development.

The enlightened report that life in the state of ignorance is still essentially a life of suffering, even though one may become king of all the worlds, for until a person recovers holistic awareness, desire is never really satisfied, and one is constantly swinging between pleasure and pain, fear and desire, and all the other pairs of opposites. One is chained eternally by the law of cause and effect to the cycle of impression, desire, action, since as long as impressions exist in one's subconscious, they reside there as the seeds of desire, which motivate a person to act for egocentric ends, which, in turn, gives rise to new impressions or deepens old one's.

Only when a person realizes that nothing in the temporal world will ever satisfy the desire for the eternal, and that nothing in the changing world will ever satisfy the desire for peace and tranquility, does a person act to break the vicious cycle in which fragmented awareness is enmeshed

Integral to awakening individuals to the need for escape from this wheel of cause and effect is proper education. Proper education is culture, for "culture" means "refinement." Under the refining influence of culture, of which religion is an essential element, the individual becomes more refined, and becomes capable of enough discrimination to begin to pursue a spiritual path.

One force of religion which is particularly helpful in this regard lies in the concept of righteousness. Initially, this concept of righteousness is conveyed through the code of conduct that embodies right living in moral precepts. Through religious and cultural training, the evolving individual learns to have remorse for relapses into unrighteousness and to mend inappropriate ways. Nevertheless, old and deep impressions are sometimes difficult to overcome through the force of will alone, especially since the willpower of the unregenerate is often weak, and backsliding is typical.

One approach to counteract backsliding is through a *mythos* of divine retribution, which history shows has often had a powerful and effective influence in preserving cultural norms. The average person was fairly well controlled by "the fear of God," and only the criminal element needed stronger sanctions. Now that humanity has evolved beyond its more primitive stages, we no longer have need of such a cultural myth, which is dependent on an anthropomorphic conception of a deity who is both arbitrary as a lawmaker and vengeful as a judge. With humanity evolving into a gentler and softer phase, a more intelligent and compassionate path can be followed.

Spiritual and religious techniques provide a degree of upliftment helpful in overcoming addictions to unrighteousness, thereby assisting those evolving to break the vicious cycle of impression, desire, action, and consequent deepening impression. Spiritual technology which is capable of exposing a person to holistic awareness found to be perhaps the most effective antidote to the vicious cycle, because the latent impressions, the seeds of egocentric thought and action, get roasted in the fire of spiritual knowledge. Moreover, even a taste of holistic awareness puts a person on the right path and whets the appetite for more and more of this experience. This is why sages of many traditions recommend right meditation as so important for spiritual growth (Cf. *Bhagavad Gita* 4 36-39; *Tao Te Ching LVI;*

Sryttanipata, 920)

Religious rites also have a purifying influence. Frequent participation at the rites is a powerful means in itself. For Catholics, the Holy Eucharist is especially potent. The effect of the rites becomes all the more powerful when put in the context of a holy life, which is perhaps no more comprehensively recommended than by Buddha in the Eightfold Noble Path – Right Appreciation, Right Thinking, Right Speech, Right Action, Right Livelihood, Right Will, Right Mindfulness, and Right Meditation.

In addition, there is in the Christian tradition a sacrament particularly well suited to the establishment of righteousness, namely Absolution. Jesus made much of it during his own lifetime, when he compared the healing of the soul to the healing of the body, and demonstrated to the dismay of his onlookers that the soul could be healed, though invisibly, just as the body could be healed visibly (Matthew 9: 1-8).

The sacrament of Absolution is freely granted to all who wish to receive it. It is regularly included in the liturgy of the Holy Eucharist. Auricular confession and penance are not the common practice with us, but are optional for those desiring it.

HOLY UNCTION AND HEALING

The sacrament of Holy Unction is made available through the Service of Healing. The sacrament of Holy Unction is for the purpose of healing both soul and body, that is, making them whole. Therefore, we find it expedient to dispense this sacrament freely in ordinary circumstances, in addition to particular situations involving either spiritual or physical affliction. The form of the healing service includes praying over the person to be healed, anointing with oil and laying on of hands in the name of Our Lord Christ, in accordance with ancient tradition (Mark 6:13).

The sacrament of Holy Unction is also an initiation into the mystery of self-transcendence. To heal is to make whole again. What needs healing? That which has fallen from wholeness. Original sin and divine redemption are symbolic ways of indicating the fall of the soul from the wholeness of Spirit and its return to wholeness through spiritual development. Healing is the symbol of this spiritual liberation.

Healing is not "merely" a symbol, however. In spiritual science, the symbol actually has greater reality than the physical or mental thing which is symbolized. In healing, for instance, it is not simply that the body is cured or made better again. For in the light of metaphysics, the body is not separate and distinct from the soul and the soul is not separate and distinct from the Spirit.

Spirit is the unitary source from which the soul shoots forth, so to speak, as a ray, and the body is the congealed energy of the soul at the grosser levels of existence. It is only through intelligence clouded by ignorance and lack of spiritual vision that anyone takes separateness to be real. The real healing, therefore, is the overcoming of spiritual ignorance, ignorance of one's true nature as the one Self of all. The healing of the body prefigures the healing of the soul (Matthew 9:1-8).

Many forms of healing are possible. Holy Unction is a sacrament; hence, directly connected to the spiritual power of Our Lord Christ through the ministry of His vicar, the duly ordained priest. However, we recall from the Gospel report that even others who were not disciples of Christ healed successfully in His name, without His explicit direction or consent. When questioned about the propriety of this, Jesus sanctioned it (Mark 9:37-38; Luke 9:49-50).

This is an instance of the "charisms" that occur independently of the sacramental tradition. Charismatic healing is a phenomenon in many denominations of Christianity, in other religions and in metaphysical circles. Some find that the gift of healing comes spontaneously or as a byproduct of their spiritual exercises or devotion. Others develop it through special practices.

Recently, scientific research has shown that virtually everyone has "therapeutic touch." These results are reported and the techniques described by a pioneer nurse, Janet Macrae, *Therapeutic Touch: A Practical Guide*. The energy field of the body can be influenced by the energy field of another and this influence can be regulated by the mind of the practitioner of therapeutic touch.

Self-healing through such practices as meditation, affirmation, and imagery are now gaining both medical and popular acceptance, although spiritual and religious healers have been using and recommending them for a long time. For example, since the mind and body are intimately connected through the nervous system, one might hypothesize that exposure to holistic awareness would also have a holistic effect on the entire mind-body relationship, or better, the total psychophysical continuum.

Recent scientific research testifies to the validity of this hypothesis. The Transcendental Meditation and TM-Sidhi program is a nonsectarian meditation practice adapted from the Vedic Shankaracharya tradition by the Hindu monk, Maharishi Mahesh Yogi. Since 1970, TM as it is called, has been the subject of voluminous scientific research. This research, much of it published in professional journals, has shown that regular practice produces beneficial results in such a variety of ways that this meditation can justifiably be called holistic in its healing effects. The conclusion can only be that healing extend beyond the province of what we have come to think of as "medicine."

Healing is a most important level of spiritual science, in that it dramatizes not only the intimate connection between mind and body, but also the physical implications of metaphysics. Those who are dominated by, or still under the influence of, the senses find their skepticism diminishing in the face of obvious results of spiritual and metaphysical healing.

The Service of Healing makes the healing power of Our Lord Christ available in a special way through the sacramental rites. The priest need not be a charismatic healer for a profound spiritual effects to take place, which may also be translated into a material effect. This spiritual healing is an important compliment to other healing methodologies, and it is made available to all who desire it. There is also a special rite for those near death.

HOLY MATRIMONY

Marriage as a social institution is virtually ubiquitous and in most cultures it is formally recognized through rites. It is clear from the Gospels and the attitude of the apostles that Jesus regarded marriage as a spiritual initiation and not simply a legal institution or a cultural fiction.

The sacrament of Holy Matrimony is an initiation into a spiritual level in which two physically distinct individuals become a single spiritual person. Spiritual levels progress in the direction of expansion and inclusion. At the supreme level there is only one Being, completely expanded and all inclusive, omnipresent and all-pervasive.

Through love, we leave the confines of our own limitations and extend our being to include that of another. In Holy Matrimony we receive an initiation into the life of love that takes us beyond ourselves, unites us with another, and gives us access to the creative power of God as we cooperate with Mother Nature to embody the souls of our children and guide them on their spiritual path.

The matrimonial state is in itself a most powerful ongoing spiritual exercise. The limitations of individuality must constantly be overcome through social cooperation. Moreover, love of one's spouse takes one outside oneself continually, as does the love of the children. In their children, individuals see the manifestation of themselves and the one they love most, in physical form.

The sacrament of Holy Matrimony is provided to all who sincerely request it, whether members of our church or not. The Ascension Alliance sets no conditions on its reception.

BAPTISM

Baptism is a sacrament of spiritual initiation and a rite of induction into formal membership in Christ's church. No profession of belief is required for membership in The Ascension Alliance, only the sincere desire "to follow Christ." The baptism with water is the outward sign of the baptism of the Spirit, which is the interior conversion of the soul to a life of faith and trust in God and an abandoning of sole reliance on the world's power and resources.

The story of Cornelius, relating the spontaneous descent of the Holy Spirit on the Gentiles, dramatizes this (Acts 10: 1-48). Fervently desiring to follow Our Lord, Cornelius petitioned the apostle Peter to come to them. As Peter was speaking to them, the Holy Spirit descended upon them and they began to manifest charisms, just as the apostles had done at Pentecost. Peter exclaimed to the Hebrew Christians who had accompanied him "Can anyone refuse the water to baptize these [because they are Gentiles], seeing that they have received the Holy Spirit just as we did?" (Acts 10:47).

Of all the sacraments, none is more emphasized in the Gospels than Baptism. The import of Jesus' words concerning Baptism make it clear that this sacrament is an initiation into the life of the Spirit. It is an initiation in the sense that there occurs an actual connection to a spiritual force, which is the Spirit of God Itself. The charismatic nature and radical transformation effected by the Baptism of the Holy Spirit is appreciated and emphasized by some Christian sects more than others. There can be no doubt that the phenomenon experienced initially and sustained by some is a true conversion, in the sense of being "born again into the life of the Spirit." However, there is a difference in metaphysical reality between a true spiritual rebirth and emotional mood-making, needing constant pumping up.

In addition, some curious lore has grown up around baptism to the effect that reception of the external form of the sacrament wipes out the spiritual detriment and metaphysical consequences of all past action in a person's life. Sometimes, baptism was even put off until late in life to take advantage of this "indulgence."

Despite such eccentricities, history is replete with instances of new Christians being born again in the Holy Spirit, some rivaling in intensity the conversion experience of the apostle Paul. The effects of this spiritual rebirth are at times dramatically attested to by healings and other charisma but the greatest proof is in the changed life that the reborn exhibit.

The life of faith is the living proof of reception of the sacrament of Baptism, whether it is accompanied by water or not. This phenomenon of spiritual rebirth is, of course, not restricted to Christianity, but rather is equally available to all sincere seekers in all times and places. Certainly, it is the characteristic of the saints and sages, wherever they are found.

In this sense, the sacrament of Baptism is the initiation into higher knowledge, which is made manifest through the Spirit of Truth. The notion of salvation through divine grace simply means that while Truth seeks out those who are open to it, there is nothing a metaphysically limited being can do to force it to come about. Our task is to make ourselves ready. Devotion to truth and performance of good works for their own sake are the external proof of this openness.

Baptism occurs consciously when a person is born again in the Spirit and steps into the life of faith, placing complete trust in God and accepting everything as a divine gift. Receiving the baptism with water does not necessarily effect this conscious transformation, although it may. Regardless of whether it does or not, reception of the sacrament of Baptism not only indicates a willingness to cooperate with divine grace to receive the Spirit, but also cleanses the spiritual channels in preparation for this rebirth.

Traditionally, the sacrament of Baptism is administered in the Catholic church only once, unlike the practice of some sects who renew their fervor and spiritual commitment on a regular basis. Catholics are welcome to renew their Baptismal commitment and we leave this up to individuals to decide for themselves. If unsure as to whether they have validly received the sacrament of Baptism people may be baptized conditionally, or "sub conditione."

CONFIRMATION

Confirmation is a sacrament whereby the spiritual aspirant is strengthened by a special infusion of the Holy Spirit, hearkening to the descent of the Spirit of God upon the apostles in "tongues of fire" on Pentecost (Acts 2:1-4). Just as the apostles are taken to have received a special initiation into the life of Spirit in addition to their baptism, so too this same initiation is preserved in the sacrament of Confirmation. Since it is an advanced initiation into the life of the Spirit, we follow tradition by reserving Confirmation to those who have already received the sacrament of Baptism.

The importance of the sacrament of Confirmation is attested to by the change reported in the disciples at the descent of the Holy Spirit upon them. Fearful and unsure before, even though they had lived constantly in the presence of Jesus, some for several years, they were transformed into fearless spiritual leaders and charismatic evangelists.

The sacrament of Confirmation is the initiation which cleanses the channel of the Spirit even more deeply than Baptism. The result of Baptism is faith, hope and love, the fundamental Christian virtues. The effect of Confirmation is prudence, justice, self-mastery, and fortitude, the plenitude of Christian virtue.

Like the sacrament of Baptism, the sacrament of Confirmation is an initiation to a higher spiritual plane. The life of this plane, characterized by "virtue," the true meaning of which is "higher power," may dawn at the time of receiving the sacrament, or its onset may be gradual as the channel is cleansed over time.

The fact that the sacrament of Confirmation is (with exception) administered by bishops indicates that it is of greater spiritual power than that of Baptism and emphasizes that it is the same initiation received by the disciples at Pentecost, as Jesus had promised. The only sacrament other than Confirmation whose administration is reserved to bishops is Holy Orders. In both cases, the initiations received are advanced and profound, for they affect not only the person, but also what the person can accomplish spiritually in the world as a servant of the Master, Our Lord Christ. The sacrament of Confirmation is traditionally received only once. If there is a question of validity, the sacrament may be readministered conditionally.

HOLY ORDERS

The sacrament of Holy Orders provides special initiation into the service of Our Lord Christ and is available to all qualified members who feel a calling to devote themselves to Christ in this intimate way. It is not necessary to feel called to the priesthood to begin reception of minor orders. Each order is an initiation in itself, with its own value. One can proceed at one's own pace, receiving as many orders as one wishes and for which one meets the qualifications.

We receive as applicants for Holy Orders all sincere persons, irrespective of age, gender, marital status, sexual orientation, or national origin. The celibate priesthood is a later innovation of some rites, to which we need not conform ourselves. The early church permitted clergy to marry, as is generally the case in the Orthodox rites today.

The Pauline prejudice against women in the sanctuary reflects a historical and cultural bias that we regard as no longer appropriate (1 Corinthians 11:3-16; 1 Timothy 2:8-15). Only men were allowed to speak in the synagogue during the time when Paul is said to have offered his opinion, and the Jewish priesthood was exclusively male. Of course, it is also argued that Jesus, the paradigmatic priest, was also a man.

Some claim that the admission of women to Holy Orders jeopardizes the validity of the rites, and that the consecration of women vitiates the apostolic succession. We dismiss this objection as groundless, and the reasoning it is based on as specious. We maintain that men and women are spiritually equal and that Holy Orders pertain to the spirit, not to the body.

Moreover, to many with the ability to notice subtle effects the efficacy of rites performed by ordained women is not impaired, although the expression of spiritual power through the mediation of women is reported to be somewhat different in its expression from that expressed through the mediation of men, due perhaps to differences in their subtle bodies. Again, ordinations and consecrations performed by women bishops are also reported by these clairvoyants to be fruitful.

The fact is that Jesus Himself broke with tradition by accepting women as disciples and allowed them to participate fully. We feel that we are reversing a trend that has grown up counter to the example of Jesus Himself.

The bias against women in virtually all cultures has been strong to the present day. It was not until the 20th century that women were admitted to suffrage in the United States, and we are only too aware that the Equal Rights Amendment to the U. S. Constitution failed to pass.

We seek to redress this unfortunate prejudice, which we believe to be without spiritual foundation. God is neither male nor female. In God, we are all created equal. If women can rise to sainthood, and even suffer martyrdom for Christ, should they not also be admitted to the benefits of advanced initiations and be given the opportunity to serve their beloved Master in this special way. We may speculate as to whether there would have been so many religious wars and inquisitions if women had held high places in the hierarchy.

The Server – The first step on the path to the sacrament of Holy Orders is admission to the sanctuary as a Server. Minor orders are received prior to major orders. The minor orders are: Cleric, Doorkeeper, Reader, Healer-Exorcist and Acolyte. The major orders are: Sub-deacon, Deacon, Priest, and Bishop.

The minor orders are initiations that foster the development of the spiritual vehicle, while the major orders clear the channel of sacramental efficacy, which is fully opened at ordination to the priesthood. Consecration to the episcopacy initiates one into the power of being able to confer these initiations upon others, just as the Holy Spirit conferred them on the apostles and the apostles conferred them on their successors (Acts 1:15-26).

While the role of Server is not a religious order, it is a momentous initiation, carrying with it great privilege and great responsibility. The initiation of Server carries with it great cleansing power and the bestowal of an immense blessing. This purification and consecration is necessary to prepare an aspirant to enter into the sanctuary, traditionally a place reserved only for adepts.

In the Temple of the Hebrews only the High Priest, according to the Law, was permitted to enter into the Holy of Holies and to have access to the Tabernacle. The sanctuary of the church, which houses the altar at which the sacrifice of the Mass is offered and the Tabernacle containing the Eucharistic Presence, is the Holy of Holies of the New Covenant. To be present in this place during the performance of the holy rites is surely an extraordinary privilege. Servers of sensitivity report that the effect is most salubrious.

Christianity is a religion of love and love is manifested in service. To serve at the altar is a most appropriate way to manifest one's love for God. Great growth is experienced through this service and one's close physical proximity reflects one's growing spiritual closeness to God.

Order of Cleric – The order of Cleric involves a special dedication of oneself to God and to the service of Christ. This is a true ordination, after the manner of the apostles, involving a praying over and laying on of hands by the ordaining bishop (Acts 6:6) or archpriest (when authorized). At this time, the ordinand receives the white alb of purity, signifying the inner initiation. At this first level the body is refined and sublimated. The alb is the outward sign of putting on the glorified body of the resurrected Christ. A first step in spiritual evolution is to know: I am not the body. A final step is to discover that the body, indeed all material existence, is of the same substance as the Self. There is ultimately no distinction between material and immaterial. All is one in the unitary Self of I AM.

Order of Doorkeeper – The second ordination is to the order of Doorkeeper. This initiation relates to transforming the emotions. The emotions of the unregenerate are similar to those of an animal lacking intelligence and spirituality. Such people are driven to unrighteous acts by their unbridled desires and ethical action is very difficult for them. When the emotions come under control lust and greed give way to spiritual contentment, and irascibility is replaced by tranquility. Righteousness becomes no longer a struggle, but rather is quite natural.

A subtler step in spiritual evolution is to recognize, namely the realization that we are not our feelings. For feelings are very powerful and can easily overshadow weak awareness of the Self. A final step in spiritual evolution is to see that the Self has an affective aspect to its nature, the predominate character of which is bliss. Bliss is the love of the Self for itself in the unity with God.

Order of Reader (Lector) – The third ordination is to the order of Reader. This initiation relates to the transformation of the intellect. The intellect of the unregenerate is clouded by identification with its object, so that one cannot discriminate one's own true nature. One goes about always focusing the attention outwardly on a myriad of objects, ever pursuing an elusive satisfaction, ignorant of the divinity within, like a millionaire dreaming he is a beggar.

Initiation into the order of Reader activates a transformation of the intellect in the direction of discrimination. The object of discrimination is to be able to distinguish that which changes from that which does not change. What changes comes to be and ceases to be; therefore, it is not fully real. What does not change is eternal; it alone can claim full reality, for how can what comes and goes be said to be truly "real" and not just a shadow passing across true substance. The enlightened testify that what does not change is the state of transcendental awareness; what moves is the mind.

Thus, an effect of increasing discrimination is the ability to perceive not only that the real "I" is not the body. Nor the emotions. It is not even the mind. In this way, a further step on the path is to know: I am not the mind, nor any of its faculties, such as the intellect.

Order of Healer (Exorcist) – The fourth ordination is into the order of Healer-Exorcist. This initiation relates to the transformation of the will. The healer heals through his intention, and intention is an operation of the will. Intention is basic to righteousness. Since human beings have freedom of will they can use this freedom either for self-aggrandizement or for noble intentions. They can intend primarily their own good at the expense of others, or they can intend the larger good of the whole. The healer focuses the will on producing wholeness of life in others, for to heal means to make whole.

To use an analogy from the movie, *Star Wars*, the exorcist deals with "the dark side of the Force," symbolized mythologically by Satan, who is pictured as pitting his mighty will against that of the Almighty, his Creator, when he said, "I will not serve." The healer allies himself with the Light against the darkness, where the Light is the holistic awareness, and darkness is taken to be the symbol of spiritual ignorance – restriction to individuality and fragmented awareness. The will is the rational appetite and as such is the seat of the higher sensibilities as opposed to the sensuous desires. The will is the field of love, along with its opposite, hate. Transformation of the will involves culturing the heart, which finds perfection in devotion and commitment to selfless service.

Through the transformation of the will we come to experience ever purer degrees of love. Love is spiritual knowledge par excellence; for God is not known directly in concepts, but rather is grasped initially in love.

Since its object is love, will is very close to spirit. Yet, will is still individual, whereas one's true nature is universal. One must come to an appreciation that will is an instrument at the service of something higher, and come to know, therefore, that I am not the will.

Order of Acolyte – The fifth ordination is to the order of Acolyte. This initiation involves the transformation of the ego. The unregenerate take themselves to be the limited ego, unaware that the boundaries of the ego are self-imposed. Through spiritual discipline the boundaries of the ego are rolled back and we come to discover ourselves as we really are – the Higher Self, I AM.

The Acolyte is a server of the priest at the rites. "Acolyte" means follower. The Acolyte obediently submits himself or herself to the discipline of the rite, in accordance with the direction of its leader, the priest, who takes the place of Christ. The ego is purified of its egocentricity through obedience to a higher authority. It humbles itself in the face of a more exalted one.

This self-effacing attitude in worldly affairs is the symbol of the interior condition of transcending boundaries on the inner planes. Just as the ego places itself outside itself through obedient service, instead of puffing itself up with pride, so too, the soul gives up more restricted levels of attainment for ever more expanded levels, until it reaches the expanded level of I AM.

The ego is our individualized existence. Since it lacks universality, it is yet fragmented and incomplete from the perspective of holistic awareness. Thus, a further step of growth involves knowing: one's true nature is not the individual ego.

The order of Acolyte is the last of the minor orders, which, as initiations, are concerned with accomplishing the transformation of the individual into a spiritual being. Once a person has been spiritually prepared, then he or she is ready to advance into major orders.

The Major orders – The major orders, as initiations, are concerned with preparing the aspirant to become a vicar of Christ, that is a replica, as it were, of the universal individual. The major orders are symbolic of the stages of holistic awareness.

In addition, the priest is one who actually ministers at the rites. A minister is one who administers in the place of the presiding officer. As Christ's minister, the priest takes on the role of the Christ in performing the rites, all of which are performed in His name and with His spiritual power. As a channel for this tremendous energy, the priest must be adequately attuned. The major orders, as initiations, culture this attunement, in conjunction with the candidate's spiritual exercises.

The Sub-deacon – The first major order is that of Sub-Deacon. Ordination as a Sub-Deacon begins the transformation of the aspirant, purified and sanctified by the previous initiations, into a priest of the Lord. This first initiation sets the stage for more profound transformations soon to take place.

The Sub-deacon begins to learn the priestly functions firsthand by taking his place at the altar and assisting in the performance of the rites. He wears a set of sacred vestments, which signify that he is a candidate for the priesthood and configures his spiritual energy, focusing it powerfully on the task at hand.

The Sub-deacon, however, has no actual priestly functions. His presence is as a witness, so to speak. This "witness" state of consciousness is the first stage of higher states of consciousness, in which one abides in one's own true nature, unencumbered by false beliefs, such as, "I am the body," "I am the mind," etc. One simply enjoys the silence of holistic awareness and witnesses the activity of Nature from which one is now separate. That is to say, the ceaseless activity of Nature, in which the ignorant are bound up, no longer overshadows Self-realization.

The Deacon – The second major order is that of Deacon. It is one of two orders specifically referred to in the New Testament, originally in connection with supervision charity work. Ordination as a Deacon effects a level of transformation which allows the candidate for the priesthood to begin the priestly way of life. The Deacon receives the stole to signify this passage from the life of the private individual to one yoked in the service of God. The Deacon is deemed sufficiently empowered by this initiation to administer the sacrament of Baptism, to handle the sacred vessels, and to distribute the Holy Eucharist.

The stage of higher consciousness symbolized by the Deacon is that in which the "witness consciousness," gets involved with the activity of Nature without losing holistic awareness. The Deacon takes on priestly functions and is given a "speaking part" in the performance of the rites, symbolizing the growing involvement of holistic awareness with Nature, in the process of discovering that at their source, inner and outer are one. Silence is discovered to have activity as its nature.

In the state of Self-knowledge, the subject knows itself as its own object, in a process of infinite self-referral. Holistic awareness flows within itself, and its flow is the source from which all activity proceeds. The silent witness growing into this knowledge comes to appreciate the activity of Nature as an intimate reality of indescribable beauty.

The Priest – The third major order is that of Priest. Ordination as a Priest effects a most profound transformation. At the time of this initiation, the candidate is empowered by the Spirit to assume the role of the Christ, the eternal High Priest, by performing the sacred rights in His name. Through a life of giving, the priest grows ever stronger spiritually, as the initiation he received deepens his connection with the higher spiritual planes and increasingly unifies him with his Master, Our Lord Christ.

The Priest symbolizes a mature state of Self-realization, in which holistic awareness knows that its nature is one, i.e., that the true nature of subjectivity is not separate from Nature, but rather that holistic awareness is not only the source and ground of all that is, but also is the very being of all that is. This is the truly universal individual – I AM WHO AM (Exodus 3:14). Knowledge of this reality confers mature realization of God within.

The Bishop – The fourth major order is that of Bishop. Consecration as a Bishop makes a priest a successor to the apostles, just as the disciple Matthias was chosen to fill the place among the original twelve left empty by the defection and death of Judas (Acts 1:15-26). Initiation as a Bishop effects perhaps the most profound transformation of all; for it empowers a priest not only to ordain others into Holy Orders, but also to consecrate other bishops, just as the apostles did. In this way the apostolic succession ever renews the clergy and perpetuates the public ministry of Jesus. In addition, the sacrament of Confirmation, being an initiation into the Pentecostal descent of the Spirit, is also traditionally administered by bishops. Thus, the Bishop symbolizes the creative outpouring of Spirit. Holistic awareness, although it is eternal and unchanging, is internally dynamic and creative within itself, comparable to "an ocean without shores," which swells within itself in waves of love. The Bishop symbolizes the creative energy of holistic awareness that is the source of all activity, and also the creative intelligence that directs all change in an orderly and evolutionary fashion.

Indeed, the episcopacy has overtone's of being an administrative office, and from the earliest times, bishops were the organizers and administrators of the churches. However, bishops are much more than religious executives.

Jesus had many devoted disciples, some of whom followed Him faithfully for His whole public life, yet the Gospels record that He selected from among them only twelve as apostles, whom He treated in a special way and kept close to Him always. Jesus did not train the apostles to be administrators, although this lot apparently fell to them later. Rather, Jesus emphasized their pastoral function and especially their evangelical mission.

The apostles originally ordained others to lesser orders (i.e. deacons), in order to keep themselves free for prayer and evangelism (Acts 6:1-6). Maintaining their contact with the Spirit by means of prayer, they would go and teach all nations, as the Master directed. This is the spiritual heritage of the bishop.

Christianity is evangelical and we take up this sacred mission, urged to do so strongly by Jesus. We interpret this mission as other than evangelical however. For we seek not to convert others to our persuasion, but rather to inspire them to the life of the Spirit.

In our view, the Spirit works from within the hearts of all people. Christ brought a message, which the world still needs to hear, about how the Spirit may be enlivened in the people's hearts. Our evangelical purpose is to enliven the Spirit in the hearts of All, and not to increase our congregations.

We see no reason why people of another Christian denomination or of another persuasion altogether might not be touched by one of us. Neither do we see any reason why they should therefore join us. It is enough that they awaken to the life of the Spirit and enjoy it wherever they are. If they are attracted to our mode of life and worship, of course, they are welcome.

All religions and denominations are aspects of the one true way, differing in form but not in substance. Cultural form is important to life in the world and people need not be torn from their accustomed ways, but simply awakened to the spiritual core of their own path. We especially decry the missionaries' practice of violating a prevailing culture under the pretext of fostering religion.

There is no reason why a Jew cannot awaken to the Spirit through an appreciation of Christ's message and not remain faithful to Judaism. After all, did not Christ Himself say that He came not to destroy the Law, but to fulfill it? (Matthew 5:17). Jesus did not contravene or abolish the Law, but only criticized a legalistic interpretation of it. Jesus, all the apostles and first disciples were Hebrews, and they kept to the spirit of the Torah, even though subsequently the Gentiles were allowed to keep to their own customs without following the precepts of the Law (Acts 10: 1-48; 15:1-32).

We find no more contradiction in Hindus, Buddhists or Taoists being vivified by Christ's message than we do Christians being uplifted by Hindu, Buddhist or Taoist principles and practices, especially their mystical and metaphysical aspects. Christ's message is equally applicable to all people, for it is a message of life in the Spirit. Similarly, Christians can take instruction from Hindu, Buddhist, Taoist, Jewish, Islamic, shamanistic and other holy people regarding their own spiritual growth and practice, just as they can from the various metaphysical and philosophical traditions. Let us adopt what is useful.

As the world grows smaller through the development of transportation and communications technology, different traditions are influencing each other. This presents the opportunity for an evangelism which recognizes both the value of what we have to offer and also what we can ourselves gain. A great leavening is taking place through the action of the Holy Spirit and a single world culture is rapidly arising, bringing with it the promise of world peace.

The contribution of Christianity to this culture can be extremely salutary and the contribution of other influences can have a profound influence on Christianity. Over the centuries, Christianity has absorbed many different cultural influences that have enhanced its richness of expression, while maintaining its essence intact.

Externally, we are very far today from that first community that convened in the upper room. Yet, hopefully, we are imbued by the same degree of spiritual intensity felt by the apostles and disciples when the Spirit descended upon them.

The ongoing challenge for the bishops, as well as for us all is to maintain the Spirit lively in the church while keeping pace with human development. The old wine must not be put into new bottles.

The bishops also replicate themselves by bringing up other qualified people through Holy Orders, training them for Christ's service, and giving them spiritual practices that allow them to make the most of the power they receive from their initiations. For initiations have their effect on the spiritual planes; yet, spiritual forces must be integrated with in one's worldly life, if a person is to gain the full benefit of them. Initiations open the channels, so to speak, and spiritual practices stimulate the flow.

In order to ensure the continuing efficacy of the rites, we require candidates for Holy Orders to be in general agreement with our *Statement of Principles* and to complete a program equivalent to a Master of

Divinity degree at Ascension Theological College is an affiliate of the Ascension Alliance, which administers the seminary program that may culminate in ordination. They participate as members of their own formation committee, comprised of a representative of the program, themselves, and at least one other member of their choosing.

The program articulates fundamental areas of knowledge all candidates must be proficient in, but allows candidates to pursue their studies in a highly decentralized way. Allows them to prepare for ministry in a variety of venues: e.g. distance learning courses, mentorship, workshops, retreats, and courses offered by other institutions.

Liturgy

The sacraments are dispensed by the church through sacramental rites, the liturgy of which is derived from scripture and tradition. While The Ascension Alliance authorizes alternative expressions of these rites, it is careful to preserve the form of the ritual and rubrics with respect to the essentials. In addition to the sacramental rites, the liturgy of The Ascension Alliance includes the Benediction of the Most Blessed Sacrament and the Divine Office, as well as hymns, blessings and other prayers. Musical accompaniment is also counted as part of the liturgy.

Since liturgical practice has an important bearing on the efficacy of the rites, the liturgy is under the direction of the bishops of the Ascension Alliance, who take counsel with the Presiding Bishop and CEO. The liturgy of The Ascension Alliance is conservative in the sense that it conforms to the due and ancient form of tradition in order to insure the efficacy of our rites.

According to ancient tradition, the rituals and rubrics have an essential connection to the spiritual dimension, such that when they are used with intent by a duly authorized person, in the Catholic and Orthodox traditions, an ordained priest, then they unfailingly produce their effects. This is not some kind of positive "magic," in the derogatory sense of "superstitious nonsense."

However, it is a form of "high magic," in the sense that the ritual and rubrics are held to be essentially connected to the form, or essence, of what they name. For example, in the Holy Eucharist, the words of consecration, when uttered by a priest with the intent to consecrate, result in the transubstantiation of the bread and wine into the Body and Blood of Our Lord Christ.

This notion that name is essentially connected to form is characteristic of the most ancient religious practice. In the world's oldest living tradition, the Vedic *rishis* or seers cognize in their yogis state of divine union that the *richas* or sacred hymns reside in the *akshara,* which means both "the alphabet," and "the eternal awareness of the Godhead." In that state of Unity, name and form are found to be one, so that their cognition of how to use the names properly in the rituals allows them to directly affect the world of form as is reported in the Vedic literature.

The Vedic concept of "mantra" signifies a sound whose proper use, when charged with power by one with the requisite authority, yields a predictable effect. In the Vedic tradition, there are mantras available for many uses, but the "key" mantras are those whose proper use leads the initiate on to holistic awareness, the yogi's state of divine union, which is the home of both the mantras and the science of their proper use, as well as being the source or the authority for charging them with power.

Similarly, in the Hebrew tradition, the name of the Lord could be written down as the sacred tetragrammaton, YHWH but was not to be pronounced aloud. At the esoteric level of understanding, this is out of respect for the holiness of the name of the Lord; however, on the esoteric level it was understood by the ancients that this name, revealed in the *mythos* by the Lord Himself was *in itself* the essence of His Divine Nature, expressed a mantric formula. Only the initiate into the divine mysteries is taught the proper pronunciation of the tetragrammaton, and only for the initiate does the expression become charged as the true Name, which is capable of leading to a personal revelation of the Lord in a meditative state.

This notion of the identity of name and form in the Godhead is common to many other mystical and metaphysical traditions. It is found, for example, in the Platonic and Neoplatonic "philosophies," which considered philosophy not as a speculative system but a way of life leading to wisdom. The identity of name and form is also found in the Egyptian mystical tradition, which also extends into prehistory.

Surrounded by peoples in whom this notion of the identity of name and form is found, we might expect to find it also in the Palestine of the first century. indeed, the idea of the intrinsic connection of name and form in the Godhead is also found in the earliest Christian records, not only the more obviously gnostic material but also in canonical works, such as the Gospel of John, whose famous prologue is a forceful statement of this view, "In the beginning was the Word, and the Word was with God; and the Word was God. All things were made through him and without him was made nothing that has been made" (John 1: 1-3).

Historians debate as to where this idea of name and form arose originally, but mystics would say that it is grounded in experiential knowledge. Being internal to the structure of holistic awareness, knowledge of the identity of name and form arises in every spiritual tradition which conduces to holistic awareness.

Our conclusion is that the intrinsic connection of name and form in the Godhead, the unmanifest Source of all manifestation, is the real basis of an effective liturgy. Effective liturgical rites are founded on a deep appreciation by those who crafted them, not only of the power of the word, but also of the posture, of the gesture, of the venture, and of the orchestration of ritual performance as a whole.

In the Vedic and Buddhist traditions, for example, there is an exact science of *mantra* or word, *mudra* or gesture, *yantra* or design, and *yagya* or ritual performance. So too, in the Torah precise instructions are given for the format and paraphernalia of Hebrew worship. The Christian tradition also pays careful attention to regulating the liturgy through the "canon," or ecclesiastical law.

Although variations on this "magical" view of the intrinsic connection of name and form have been espoused throughout the course history by various philosophical and esoteric schools, these views have been opposed by the "nominalist" position, which holds that the meaning of words is determined by convention alone. In fact, until recently, the predominant contemporary view had been that the meaning of a word is indeed determined by convention – that is, by the use of the word in the context of some activity. This view sees meaning arising out of common agreement among language-users, not out of any essential connection with what words refer to.

Of late, however, discoveries made in the sciences of psychology, linguistics, and psycholinguistics show that the nominalist position relates only to the level of "surface grammar," and that there is also a level of "depth grammar" with its own dynamics. At the level of depth grammar, researchers postulate an intrinsic connection between name and form, which is mediated by the very structure of human awareness through its physical expression, the nervous system. In other words, it is not by accident that language-users agree upon what they do. The conventions into which we are nurtured are grounded in the very structure of the universe, as it appears to us on the basis of our own nature, i.e., our psychophysical structure.

Therefore, we hold with the traditionalists, the esotericists, and the seers of old, as well as this branch of modern science, that there are strong grounds for asserting an intrinsic connection between name and form. hence, between the ritual and rubrics of the liturgy and the effects which proper performance produces. Accepted standards of liturgical practice are more than pious guidelines they are actually important criteria of sacramental efficacy.

Significantly, however, although Jesus Himself is held to have instituted the sacraments, He is not credited with formulating their liturgical aspects, except in a very inchoate way in comparison with the way the liturgy has developed over subsequent ages. Indeed, there are many different liturgies in use in the Catholic and Orthodox churches, determined by the canons of the various rites. So the question becomes, what liturgical standards are most appropriate?

There are areas of major agreement among the various rites concerning essential constituents of the liturgy. We have sought to observe these essentials while establishing a canon for our distinctive rite. We have also consulted the ancient sources in matters of expression, to avail ourselves of the spiritual perceptiveness of the holy one's of previous ages.

However, our liturgy also reflects the liberal stance of our church. Our rites have been designed so as not to require members of the congregation to express sentiments or convictions they may not share. Our liturgy emphasizes sanctification, blessing, praise and giving, and eschews dwelling on sin and suffering, penitence and contrition. For we feel that emotional quality goes far in establishing the spiritual consequences of worship and devotion. The Ascension Alliance maintains that unconditional positivity is the true meaning of faith, hope and love, the Christian cornerstone virtues.

Scripture

The Ascension organization takes as its scriptures the New Testament, consisting of the Four Gospels, the Epistles, the Acts of the Apostles and the Book of Revelation, and includes the noncanonical scriptures as well. The Hebrew canonical scriptures, as well as the Apocrypha and Pseudepigrapha, are recognized as antecedent to the Christian scriptures. In addition, we esteem the scriptures of all religions, as well as the expression of the saints of all ages and cultures, as valuable aids to spiritual growth.

We hold that some but not all of what is considered scripture is divinely inspired by the Holy Spirit, in the sense that those who were legitimately channels for this revelation were people of great spiritual advancement, whose intuition and awareness were established on a high plane, while other writers may not have been as spiritually aware. Even with respect to the words of the prophets and Jesus Himself, interpolations have been inserted and redactions made that biblical scholars are now discovering through sophisticated research techniques.

Contemporary historical research shows that many misconceptions concerning scripture have influenced both Judaism and Christianity. For example, it is now clear to scholars that the Pentateuch, or Torah, namely the first five books of the Hebrew scriptures were composed over an extensive period of time, and contain at least four major sources which have been redacted, or skillfully worked into each other. Richard Elliott Friedman's *Who Wrote the Bible?* is an excellent account of the scholarly research.

Until relatively recently, scholars were not permitted to suggest that the Torah was not dictated to Moses by God in its entirety, and many pious souls still believe that this is so. More importantly, however, this belief has been extremely influential in the development of Judaism and stances appeal for their justification.

The New Testament also has generally been taken as an historical account, essentially the biography of Jesus, containing His very words. Scholars now recognize that the New Testament is more confessional and kerymatic than historical – more oriented to confessing belief in the Christian faith and preaching this faith than to providing a literal account of historical facts. Moreover, contemporary scholars have shown that the New Testament is comprised of multiple sources, interpolations and redactions, and is not the work of the four evangelists as tradition would have it.

Since there is no absolute standard to differentiate in specific cases, we do not require acceptance of any aspect of scripture or any particular interpretation. Biblical scholarship and scriptural studies are valuable disciplines which are greatly expanding our knowledge and understanding. In addition, the growing body of scientific knowledge and the knowledge of the scriptures of other religions are casting ever new light on the Christian scriptures.

Many levels of meaning are included in the scriptures, principally the literal or exoteric, and the spiritual or esoteric, as well as the poetical or mythical which links them. The literal level concerns primarily the descriptive and the historical. The poetical includes the metaphorical and analogical while the spiritual level is that of the anagogical or mystical.

Much, if not most, of what is valuable in the scriptures resides at the spiritual level. This level of meaning cannot be expressed adequately at the literal level, so it is cloaked in poetry and myth, to be revealed to the aspirant on the inner planes in consequence of growing spiritual experience. As one's spiritual experience grows, one spontaneously comes to realize the hidden meaning behind certain scriptural passages and these realizations serve as landmarks and confirmations of one's spiritual advancement. The fact that the esoteric meaning of the scriptures both exists and is impenetrable by ordinary intelligence is attested to by the Gospel (Luke 24:45).

Training in metaphysics is, in our view, necessary for even a rudimentary understanding of the Bible. Metaphysics is as old as religion itself, for every ancient religion, whether Vedic, Taoist, Hebrew, Egyptian, Mesopotamian, Greek, Mayan, or shamanistic, has reference to metaphysical concepts when read from the metaphysical point of view. Metaphysics based on mystical experience finds its fulfillment in this. Since spiritual development is inherent in human nature, realized people should be found in all cultures, in all epochs. Since these are the saintly one's who were the repositories of religion, it is not surprising that every religion is discovered to contain both hints for the spiritual aspirant and an esoteric message for the more adept when examined from the metaphysical point of view.

All truly valid scripture and metaphysics relate to the mystical experiences of saints and sages. It as naive to think God dictated the utterances sometimes attributed to Him. The word, "prophet," means "to speak for." The prophet speaks not for himself, in the limited sense, but rather for the great I AM to the degree that the prophet experiences spiritual insight. True prophecy comes from a higher level of consciousness than is ordinarily experienced.

Tradition

We recognize the importance of tradition along with scripture as an internal component of the Christian revelation. The Gospels imply that Jesus taught His disciples privately more than He revealed publicly (Matthew 13:36). The Gospels are largely a record of His public ministry and even this record is truncated (John 20:30; 21:25). We assume then that traditions dating back to apostolic times may contain much of value that was passed on orally or embedded in the liturgy.

Many matters central to Christian belief and worship are conveyed through tradition. Most of Mariology, for example, is derived from tradition, as is the veneration of the saints. There are no specific liturgical requirements in the scriptures, other than brief phraseology, yet, many rites have been performed in essentially the same way for an extended period. Again, no mention is made in scripture of such central articles of Catholic belief as the assumption of the Holy Lady Mary, and yet Christian churches have recognized many matters of tradition as authentic from the earliest times. While we do not blindly accept such traditions either literally or in their entirety, we acknowledge that they are a rich repository and may contain much that is valuable, at least symbolically.

The initial period of tradition ends with the last writings of the church fathers. We regard this first period as most significant, in that it is most closely connected to Our Lord. Unfortunately, the tradition of the early church was marred by internecine warfare as the orthodox sought to extirpate what they deemed to be heresies. A great deal of the richness of early

Christian diversity was unfortunately lost in the effort to create a homogeneous "catholic" church. In examining some of this material a good case can often be made that the wrong side won. It is still not too late, however, to set right earlier mistakes in judgment.

Subsequently to the first centuries, tradition came more under external influence, especially as Christianity spread to many divers lands and peoples. Nevertheless, tradition derived from the saints, the fathers and doctors of the church and the other great Christian thinkers, including the Protestant reformers and theologians, merits consideration, along with those whom the orthodox regard as either schismatics or heretics.

We hold further that the scriptures and traditions of the other religions of the world are a fertile field of ideas and example. We feel an affinity for the mystical doctrines found there, in particular among the Islamic Sufis, the Hindu yogis, the Buddhist arahats, the Taoist sages, and the Kabbalists. For these serve to illumine the role of experience in the spiritual advancement, as well as shed the light of other mature perspectives on common themes of spirituality.

Without requiring adherence to any specific aspect of scripture or tradition, we recommend the body of the Christian revelation as a guide both for worship and for self-perfection. We further recommend that Christianity as a whole be approached in the light of all other relevant knowledge, including that of other spiritual, religious, and philosophical traditions, as well as the best of contemporary thinking and research.

The development of the Christian faith has not ended, but is an ongoing process which is driven by the inborn desire of human beings for perfection and guided by the action of the Holy Spirit operating in the hearts of seekers everywhere and at all times.

Theology and Philosophy

We neither adopt nor sponsor any theological or philosophical position, but rather recognizes that both theology and philosophy are speculative endeavors subject to the limitation of language in expressing transcendence. Language is capable of formulating conceptual models which serve as maps, so to speak. We must be vigilant to avoid the temptation to confuse the map with the territory and to take the map for the reality of what it purports to simply represent.

While theological and philosophical speculation is valuable for clarifying thought, it is incapable of conveying spiritual truth, which is necessarily experiential. Jesus came neither as a theologian nor as a philosopher, and His own teaching is significantly devoid of anything resembling such speculation. Only later was the Christian message married to Greek thought, first to that of Plato and the Neo-Platonists by the Church Fathers, and then to that of Aristotle by the Scholastic Doctors.

We affirm that inspiration exists in and can be drawn from both theology and philosophy. Study of the great thinkers will at least sharpen one's own thought processes, clarify one's ideas and reduce confusion regarding concepts and reasoning. More importantly, theological and philosophical studies put us in contact with the minds of people of great intelligence and deep spiritual insight, thereby culturing our own intellects and intuition. Whether we accept any specific position from them is immaterial in that our mental flexibility becomes greatly developed and we gain a rich background against which to formulate our own ideas and to test our thinking.

Clearly, an informed and intelligent approach to the intellectual richness available in the Christian religion is superior to a naive or careless one. We unequivocally recommend that all one's assumptions and beliefs be subject to critical scrutiny in the light of the best available information. Both theology and philosophy are valuable tools in this regard, as is science, which not long ago was called natural philosophy. Through the study of theology, philosophy and science we come to acquire not only information, but also rigorous methodology.

Instead of launching elaborate disquisition's, we prefer to maintain the Christian message in as close a form as possible to what Jesus presented, clearly distinguishing later accretions. While some of this increase may actually be due to the inspiration of the Spirit, as truly spiritual people elaborate from their experience of divinity then much of it is unmistakably cultural.

Rather than expand Christian doctrine by appeal to theology and philosophy, we recommend using theology and philosophy as tools for greater understanding of spiritual truth, just as we use the tools of biblical scholarship and scriptural studies to clarify the original material, establish its authenticity and display its contextual intent.

In view of the historical character of theology and philosophy and the influence of both science and culture on it, theology and philosophy of one era are inadequate to express the potential of a new era in human development. No one school of thought is ever either absolute or complete. While we believe that our contribution to Christian perspective is genuine and valuable for seekers today, we do not seek to establish an "Ascensionist creed" for all times. If we take any position with respect to Christian doctrine, it is an evolutionary one that sees Christianity keeping abreast the pace of human development.

Nevertheless, it would be naive to think that one can be spiritual without a theology, or take an intelligent approach to the world without a philosophy. Theology and philosophy have already shaped Christianity into what it is today, for better or for worse. It is impossible to ignore theology and philosophy, for every spiritual and religious interpretation presupposes a theological and philosophical stance. Better that we take a considered position, rather than unwittingly accept what is foisted upon us through the circumstance of our ignorance.

For example, as Elaine Pagels admirably brings to light in her book, *Adam, Eve and the Serpent,* much of what is negative and self-deprecating in Christianity is due to Augustine's later theology, which was based on his lifelong difficulties in disciplining his highly passionate temperament. He took this as a universal affliction of humankind and propounded a theology founded upon irresistible cupidity.

Augustine attributed his failing in the face of temptation to original sin. Pagels shows that Augustine's argument fails, due to an overemphasis on and even a misreading of Genesis. Augustine's eloquent rhetoric, however, assisted by contemporary sociological factors, succeeded in carrying the day and Christian doctrine subsequently taught that we are all born hopeless sinners and that nothing we can do ourselves is of any avail. Divinity within became shrouded by a cry of *mea culpa* and *miserere*.

Unless we realize the stakes and reflect for ourselves, we are likely to be caught up in such historical currents unnecessarily, and there are many of them. The point is that theology and philosophy, properly considered, are conceptual expressions of a person's deepest commitments. We refrain from imposing any particular conceptual framework on our members. All are free to come to their own conclusions. Indeed, it would be surprising if intelligent people, experiencing spiritual growth, did not find their theologies and philosophies growing along with them over their lives.

We maintain that spirituality is openness to transcendence and that spiritual development is the evolutionary path to holistic awareness which all beings are on, whether they have realized it yet, or not. We take religious expression to be largely oriented to divine worship, therefore, a matter of the heart, more than the head.

However, the intellect is a useful tool if it is kept sharp. Therefore, we heartily recommend research and study in spiritual and religious thought, as well as in all other relevant disciplines, such as science, philosophy, and the humanities.

Socrates is reputed to have said that a life not reflected upon is not worth living. We can interpret this dictum thus: we are born into a culture and environment, including our earliest impressions and our subsequent education, which inculcates us with assumptions about the most basic things. In this way we inherit a world view, rather than fashion one creatively. At a certain point, it behooves our evolution to examine our assumptions, and to take responsibility for self-creation by replacing assumptions which inhibit our growth with assumptions that foster it.

The "world" in which we live is one largely of our own making. Anyone who doubts this need only read some anthropology. Through our agreement with the others around us we fashion a world view that we take to be "reality." What we often do not realize is that other world views are not only possible, but perhaps more conducive to our evolution. The immature take their particular map for the territory it only represents.

A world view is founded on a set of hidden assumptions that the we do not even suspect are there. They take others who do not share important assumptions of theirs to be either liars, demented, or "primitive."

Historically, spiritual and religious assumptions have been determinative of some of the most fundamental aspects of a cultural world view. For example, this may be a major reason that interfaith marriages so often fail. Either the two people don't have a common enough platform of shared assumptions for effective communication regarding basic issues in life; or their assumptions clash on important issues.

Since we are a liberal organization, a cardinal principle is that an individual has the responsibility for personal growth. Therefore, we encourage freedom for self-development, and we point to the need for a liberal education to equip a person with the requisite resources and tools.

A sharp intellect and a curious mind are fundamental in this process. We recommend that a person apply these resources to cultural assumptions, including even the most sacrosanct, and to prove them in a *trial by fire,* as it were – that is, the "fire" of intelligence.

For example, the study of contemporary Biblical scholarship and archeological research will serve to rid one of many inherited assumptions that can no longer stand the test of rigorous investigation, while the complacent will needlessly continue to operate under the burden of these outmoded principles. In addition, the study of esoteric interpretations will not only replace assumptions founded on an exoteric bias with those based on a subtler appreciation, but it will also suggest new world views, expanding one's options for self-creation.

For instance, creation spirituality is now questioning the assumptions of a world view based on original sin, and replacing them with assumptions based on "original blessing," the title of an influential book by former Dominican and now Episcopal priest, Matthew Fox. Much of this new thinking is based in part on the exciting thought of Pierre Teilhard de Chardin, S.J., a modern scientist-visionary, who has propounded a mystical world view to challenge the materialistic thinking of our scientific age.

The New Thought movement in Christianity has also been responsible for shifting our cultural religious assumptions from a negative bias, emphasizing sin, guilt and suffering, to a positive bias, focusing on increasing positivity and the unfolding of divinity within in this life. In addition, the influx of eastern spirituality to the West has begun to refocus attention on the spiritual quest as one involving the development of holistic awareness – especially through the use of meditation as a spiritual methodology .

Far from being anti-intellectual we encourage all to read widely in these sources, and to employ them as resources for self-creation. The ancient meaning of "philosophy," is "the love of wisdom," and it signifies not an empty intellectual exercise, but rather, the pursuit on an intelligent *way of life,* oriented to development of full potential.

Aristotle, for example, investigated the ultimate motivation of human behavior in his *Nichomachean Ethics.* He noticed that human beings always act with some end in view, and that every proximate end could be traced to an ultimate end, namely, the pursuit of happiness.

He found, however, that people disagree over what happiness is and what will produce it. Some argue for fame, others for fortune, and still others for power. But, experience shows that nothing that comes and goes, like fame, fortune, and power, can produce lasting happiness.

Aristotle reasoned that happiness is actually not itself an ultimate. It is rather the byproduct of our biological functioning, and is found to accompany the unfoldment of full potential or excellence. The way to happiness is through the pursuit of excellence.

What is excellence for human beings? Aristotle reasoned that it cannot be something we share with the other animals, but must involve our humanity in a specific way. That which distinguishes human beings from other animals is intelligence. Excellence, then, would involve the unfoldment of the full potential of intelligence.

Aristotle investigates the various expressions of intelligence and finds them very satisfying; scientific understanding, moral uprightness, artistic appreciation, love and friendship – and all are included in a full life. These are values which reside in the spirit, and are not subject to decay. Yet, we know that age clouds the mind, we lose friends and loved one's to death, and our emotions are subject to swings, up and down. So none of these can be fully satisfying either.

Aristotle pushes on to find that the highest level of human intelligence is knowledge of the divine, which is attuned conceptually first, but then is filled in by meditative experience, culminating in self-realization. The full potential of human intelligence is the attainment of divinity within – the state of intelligence cognizing itself. All mystics describe this state as one of unfoundedness and bliss, beyond space, time and change, a state that is subject to neither diminution, nor decay.

This state, according to Aristotle, is the embodiment of philosophy and theology, the state of human excellence, and the only true happiness. We would agree, and recommend that one use the intellect judiciously to discriminate the valuable from the worthless, and to pursue that which is most valuable – divinity within.

Aristotle also noted that human beings are social beings; their lives are bound up in society. Therefore, a full life requires that we join the community, now recognized through the advent of communications and transportation technology to be "a global village."

As citizens of the world our community is worldwide. Our concept of the Christian message bids us join the pursuit of excellence together and share the contributions that our respective creativity makes possible, so that the divine within can merge with the divine without. Guided by love, let Unity be our goal.

Christian Ethics

We hold that the New Covenant is a dispensation of love rather than of law. Saint Augustine has summarized Christian ethics in one simple precept, "Love and do as you will."

When asked, which is the greatest commandment of all, Jesus responded, quoting the Torah "You shall love the Lord your God with your whole heart, and with your whole soul and with your whole mind. This is the greatest and first commandment. And the second is like it, 'you shall love your neighbor as yourself.' On these two commandments depend the whole Law and the Prophets" (Deuteronomy 6:4-5; Leviticus 19:18; Matthew 22:35-40).

Moreover, Jesus instituted a new commandment of love: "A new commandment I give you, ... that as I have loved you, you also love one another. By this all men will know you are my disciples, if you have love for one another" (John 13: 34-35). Later, Jesus made clear the extent of altruism involved in loving as He loves, when He said, "This is my commandment, that you love one another as I have loved you. Greater love than this no man has, that one lay down his life for his friends" (John 15:12-13).

Our Lord also taught us to see Himself in all persons, "Whatsoever you do to these, the least of my brethren, you do also to Me" (Matthew 25:40). Not risking to be mistaken about the universal nature of Christian charity, Jesus explicitly includes all and everyone, under even the most trying circumstances. "Love your enemies, do good to those who hate you, and pray for those who slander you" (Luke 6:27). For, He observes, "if you love those who love you, what merit have you? Even the unregenerate love those who love them" (Luke 6: 32).

In the naive view at the literal level of understanding, the basic spiritual technique of Christianity is believing intellectually in the divinity of Jesus Christ and keeping His commandments. This is essentially a holdover of the Old Testament conception of believing in Yahweh and adhering to his Law out of fear of punishment. The New Covenant is simply the replacing of Yahweh with Christ and the complicated Hebrew Law with a simplified version. In both cases, morality is fundamental; only the form of the law is different. The Christian form is simpler, in this view, because Christ has redeemed us from sin once and for all.

Taking this view to be simplistic and realizing that it is impossible to legislate love, we endeavor to look deeper into Jesus' message. We hold that Christian morality is the result of universal love.

In the absence of love, regulating behavior within certain prescribed channels is hardly more than social regulation. Even the laws of men do this. Moreover, the success of such laws is limited, even though they are enforced by material and physical sanctions.

The Christian path is the way of love. It is through love that we come to a knowledge of God, Who is Love. The insistence on love as supremely spiritual is also supremely practical: Love unites us with our divine nature. Love not only leads us to the kingdom of heaven; Divine Love, the very nature of God, is the kingdom of heaven that lies within us and among us (1 John 4:7-21). The kingdom of heaven is love, which is both within us and among us. It is potentially *within* each of us, for where does love exist, but in the heart? It is also potentially *among* us, for this love can be shared from heart to heart.

The enlightened of all spiritual traditions report that the very nature of divine union is bliss – the supremely satisfying joy of transcendental love. "God is love and he who abides in love abides in God and God in him" (1 John 4:16).

We hold that the way to true Christian love lies in freedom. Freedom is of the will and the will is the appetite of intelligence. What intelligence desires is truth. Freedom, therefore, is not simply freedom from restriction nor yet freedom to indulge. The deeper aspect of freedom is freedom for unfolding full spiritual potential which is realization of our divinity within.

The way to real love, transcending mere infatuation, is through freedom and truth. Giving ourselves and our fellows the freedom to be what we are and to become all that we can become is the prerequisite to seeking truth authentically. If within this arena of freedom we sincerely pursue truth, we will become more and more the divine being that we truly are. For, as we become more and more ourselves, unclouded by untruth, unnaturalness, and ignorance of the true Self, we come to love ourselves more and more. Loving ourselves more and more, we become more and more lovable. We and our fellows radiate love in a community that finds love growing by leaps and bounds. This is the true Communion of the Saints, the Mystical Body of Christ and the true Church. The one true religion is following the Spirit within.

Righteousness arises from being centered on spiritual development. Being established in this state of righteousness, one does not fall prey to temptation, that is, the tendency to wrongdoing, where wrongdoing is anything which detracts from spiritual advancement. Righteousness is not attainable by trying to conform oneself to a code of conduct which is concerned with the external.

Righteousness is achieved only by aligning one's being through spiritual practice with what we as Christians call the Spirit (Matthew 12:31-35; 1 Galatians 5:16-25). Taoists call this Tao, while Hindus and Buddhists call it Dharma. In each case the source of righteousness is found to be unity with the spirit of the natural law found within, rather than being constrained by the letter of an external code (Romans 2:14-15; Bhagavad Gita 2:48-51; Tao Te Ching XVIII). Jesus' condemnation of legalism makes this abundantly clear (Matthew 15:1-20). Therefore, we make no attempt to legislate Christian morality, nor to interpret it in specific situations. We simply call to attention the law of love that Our Lord Christ enjoins and to remind that the scriptures and tradition, including church doctrine, theology and philosophy are all aids in informing one's conscience with respect to specific questions and in developing individual precepts.

We do not take any stance as an institution either politically or socially, other than to recommend adherence to the basic principles of Christian ethics, namely the freedom of individual conscience, personal responsibility and Christian love. This does not imply that we recommend social complacency. We respect the free choice of individuals and leave members of the Church and clergy free to participate in political and social causes, acting on their own behalf, in accordance with the dictates of their conscience as informed by Christian principles.

The criterion of true love is action; anyone who says he loves God and does not keep His word is a liar (1 John 2: 3-6). Jesus also gave us the golden rule, "As you wish men to do to you so also do to them" (Luke 6:38). Moreover, Jesus tells us that no one has greater love than the one who lays down his life for his friend (John 15:13).

Christian love is not a mere emotional feeling; it is a true compassion that results in selfless service. This activity for a greater good than one's egocentric concerns, that is, or something that transcends the bounds of one's limited individuality, is salutary not only for the recipient of the service, but also for the one who is serving. Service is a spiritual technique, in that it takes one beyond one's limited individuality in the direction of universality.

As the philosopher Emmanuel Kant noticed, the golden rule calls each of us to act universally in our intent and action. That is to say, the golden rule requires each of us to ask whether the action we are contemplating could serve as a standard for the behavior of all others. If it can, then it is something that promotes good generally, or at least diminishes no one.

The more universal a person is, the more he or she intends and acts for the good of the whole. And in pursuing the larger good, one simultaneously achieves one's own good – spiritual evolution.

Fellowship In The Spirit

Our movement is a fellowship of followers of the Spirit. We give ourselves and each other encouragement to live the truth as we perceive it in our hearts. To live our deepest truth with integrity is to become ever more the Christ, the true Self of all and the source of real fellowship among people and nations. We hearken to the Delphic oracle, "Know thy Self" and hold high the proverb, "To thine own Self be true" knowing that as brothers and sisters in Christ we are indeed one with each other and one with Him.

Fellowship in the Spirit is unity in Divine Love. "No man is an island." As social beings, we crave community. True community implies spiritual communion, that is, heartfelt relationship. The basis of our spiritual communion is Holy Communion with and in the Lord, which unites us at our common Source.

Late Patriarch, Herman Adrian Spruit, asserted that the Church should be "connectional" rather than hierarchical, presbyterial, or congregational. We are a church of teamwork, in which we endeavor to be "all for one and one for all." Everyone is welcome as a privileged participant to any of our churches, centers, or congregations. It is a system designed to allow the stream of church life to flow with a maximum of concord.

The clergy of the Ascension movement claim no rights over their members with respect to freedom of thought, conscience, or expression. Clergy are differentiated from laity solely by their ministerial and organizational functions. The clergy of the Church are the servants. They serve quintessentially by officiating at the sacraments and other ceremonies traditionally performed by those holding valid orders, in accordance with the rules of apostolic succession. Bishops are the servants of the servants of God. Clergy in our movement do not generally charge formal fees for their ministerial services. However, since we are dependent on voluntary contributions for support, honoria and donations are gratefully accepted.

Ascension welcomes all persons to its congregations. We invite all qualified people, including ministers of other churches, to our pulpits. Ordained priests of other rites whose orders are valid in accordance with the apostolic succession are welcome to officiate or concelebrate at our altars. Our members and clergy are welcome to participate in other rites and at other opportunities for worship.

Epilogue

The Ascension Alliance finds its place among the mystical and metaphysical organizations of the world, as well as among the so-called independent, or free, Catholic churches. As a Church, we make the traditional sacraments available within the context of divine worship.

There is now growing evidence that the early Christian Church was divided in its understanding of Christ's message. Some, for example, took the "Kingdom of Heaven" as a new order on earth, others as a messianic apocalypticism, while others understood it as a gnostic mysticism. The apocryphal writings that have now surfaced suggest that many of the early believers were of the gnostic persuasion. The promise of the second coming of the risen Christ was for them the prediction of their own spiritual enlightenment, rather than an apocalyptic vision of either a new political order on earth or a heavenly rapture for the righteous.

Our Ascension organization roots itself within the tradition of Independent Catholicism, as advanced by bishops Hampton, Spruit, and Gundrey, but we now assume the mantle of a "free" Church, embracing new insights, such as those of the "Emerging Church" and "Jewish Renewal" movements, which are themselves part of a bigger movement of Spirit.

We are committed to serving the people of God within the context of a postmodern world that is rife with change and challenge – a changing world that is more in need of spiritual renewal than ever before.

It is our intent to prepare a new generation of clergy through our formation program, Ascension

Theological College. Our program is a highly decentralized program that asks candidates to assume the initiative in developing an individualized program of professional formation and personal growth in consultation with a formation committee; root themselves in Christian tradition and ministerial skills; broaden themselves through exposure to mystical traditions; and creatively innovate, adapting the best of tradition to the needs of a rapidly changing world, perhaps through innovation in the sacraments and creating new sacramentals.

We believe in the communion of saints, including the guiding lights of the contemporary era. In the tradition of Archbishops Herman Adrian and Meri Louise Reynolds Spruit; Archbishop Richard Gundrey; and others; we commit ourselves to preparing "barefoot priests" for service to our brothers and sisters. In the memory of Brother Wayne Teasdale, we now intend to support a cadre of contemplative individuals who feel called to be witnesses to the divine as "monks in the world." In the spirit of Peace Pilgrim, we now aspire to find Peace in ourselves and extend it to the rest of the world.

ABOUT ASCENSION

The Ascension Alliance and Community of Ascensionists is a religious jurisdiction and congregation; an Independent Catholic organization; part of the one Mystical Body of Christ; a Church; an umbrella religious organization; and expression of God's mystical movement of Spirit. We draw our lines of apostolic succession from the historic churches of the West and East, although we are not a part of the Roman Catholic or Eastern Orthodox churches. We derive our chief western line through the Old Catholic churches of Europe, which separated from the see at Rome in the early 1700s. Our principal eastern line comes from the ancient churches of India, which are believed to have been established by the Apostle Thomas in the year 52, C.E., and which were served by Assyrian and Syrian Orthodox bishops for generations. We like to think of ourselves as born of a "free" Catholic vision and a much larger stirring of Spirit, which beckons us to transcend old ways that no longer work, ascend to higher levels of consciousness, and be transformed. In addition, we are dedicated to helping other seekers who wish to do the same.

We Joyfully Celebrate the Sacraments in Communities Worldwide

Mailing Address:
P.O. Box 167, Vaughn, WA 98394

Website: ascensionalliance.org

www.ingramcontent.com/pod-product-compliance
Lightning Source LLC
Chambersburg PA
CBHW061947070426
42450CB00007BA/1080